Victor Hugo

Titles in the series Critical Lives present the work of leading cultural figures of the modern period. Each book explores the life of the artist, writer, philosopher or architect in question and relates it to their major works.

In the same series

Victor Hugo

Bradley Stephens

REAKTION BOOKS

For Milind, Jayan, Hazel, Iris, Nina, Lucas and Ellis,
who represent the future that Hugo strived for
and who I kept in mind when writing

Published by Reaktion Books Ltd
Unit 32, Waterside
44–48 Wharf Road
London N1 7UX, UK

www.reaktionbooks.co.uk

First published 2019
Copyright © Bradley Stephens 2019

Printed and bound in Great Britain by Bell & Bain, Glasgow

A catalogue record for this book is available from the British Library

ISBN 978 1 78914 084 2

Contents

Note on Texts and Translations

Published English translations of Victor Hugo's writing have been used where possible. All other translations are my own and refer mostly to the 45-volume Ollendorff and Albin Michel edition of Hugo's *Complete Works* (*Œuvres complètes*), ed. Paul Meurice, Gustave Simon and Cécile Daubray (Paris, 1902–52), since these volumes are freely available online should readers wish to consult them.

For full details of all the editions used in this biography and for the relevant abbreviations in the references, please see the References section at the end.

Photograph of Hugo by Nadar (Gaspard-Félix Tournachon), 1878. Perhaps
the most iconic image of Hugo, depicting him as the thoughtful elder statesman
of the French Republic.

Introduction

Victor Hugo's life can read like an epic novel. Born in 1802 and dying in 1885, he bore witness to the aspirations and anxieties of a century that continues to speak to our own. He looked on as an era of new possibilities broke fresh ground which was watered by the rush of ideologies flowing from the American and French Revolutions of the previous century.

The son of a military father, Hugo came into direct contact with the Napoleonic Wars before the age of ten. He lived through France's First Empire, the Bourbon Restoration, the July Monarchy and the Second Republic during his first fifty years. The rise of the Second Empire then forced him into almost two decades of exile before it fell in 1870, at which point he returned to France to watch the Third Republic take hold and to stare down a series of national crises. Each of these dizzying turns was instigated by historic upheaval – the Battle of Waterloo in 1815; the July Revolution in 1830; the revolutionary uprisings of 1848; the 1851 *coup d'état*; the Franco-Prussian War in 1870–71; and the 'Bloody Week' ending the Paris Commune in 1871.

Hugo believed his fate was tied to that of a century whose birth preceded his own by only two years. This broader idea of destiny was especially strong in an era whose dawn was coloured by Napoleonic adventure and Romantic genius. His name appeared to draw together different forces, auguring greatness: his Latin forename denoting victory, as well as Mediterranean connotations of classical antiquity, was coupled with the attributes of spirit signified by the family name 'Hugo' and its Saxon roots in Northern Europe. Seemingly marked out for glory, he eagerly embraced his generation's belief in the power of the individual to shape the world and make history. 'Thought is power,' he said, 'and all power is a duty.'[1]

Hugo had great hopes for his literary talents. Demonstrating an instinct for posterity that was as audacious as any would-be Bonaparte or Byron, he epitomized the French republican values of liberty, equality and fraternity. As both writer and statesman, he envisaged his country as the cradle of modern civilization, even to the point of refusing to learn English while living out his exile in the Channel Islands. He believed that France was the global standard-bearer for progressive democracy in the wake of the French Revolution of 1789, whose violence he decried but whose devotion to the social ideals of the Age of Enlightenment he extolled. His writing and politics came to exemplify the Enlightenment's thirst for encyclopaedic knowledge and its doctrines of personal and religious liberty. This universal and egalitarian spirit enabled him to commit himself to common truths and collective interests as the *grand homme* or 'great man' of nineteenth-century French letters.

His career was undeniably illustrious. He was elected as one of the so-called 'immortal' members of the Académie française shortly before his 39th birthday in 1841 and achieved recognition across the globe for his writing.[2] The writer who gave world literature one of its most bankable best-sellers in *Les Misérables* (1862), and who inspired Verdi to adapt his plays not just once but twice, had among his admirers an august list of writers – from Dickens and Dostoyevsky to Tennyson and Tolstoy. His work can be both sober and eccentric, readily filtering what he observed and what he felt. His imagination, which fought against stultifying tradition and looked beyond appearances, had much in common with the visionary mysticism of other European Romantics such as William Blake and Novalis. His deep-set eyes hinted in their intensity that he was born with the penetrating gaze of a poetic seer, even if his recurrent complaints of eye strain and soreness suggest that any such visionary powers might have come at a cost.[3]

In the same breath, Hugo was also the socially conscious arbiter of human rights who defied authoritarianism. An indomitable public servant who was elected to both the National Assembly and the Senate, Hugo committed himself to eradicating poverty, improving education, promoting international cooperation and opposing persecution. His correspondents included Garibaldi during the final decade of the Risorgimento in the 1860s. By the time of Hugo's death, he had outlasted three French kings and two emperors. Across the twentieth century, causes close to his heart became political realities, such as greater social welfare and the abolition of the death penalty in France, as well as the foundation of a union of European states.

Success did not, however, come as easily for Hugo or sit as comfortably with him as his storied reputation implies. Jean Cocteau's barb that 'Victor Hugo was a madman who thought he was Victor Hugo' pokes fun at the poet's sense of self-importance,[4] but it ignores how Hugo never fully believed his own hype as the benchmark for other writers to be measured against. His ego could be as circumspect as it was bombastic. Although the name 'Victor Hugo' suggests a bold ability to bring separate traits and spaces together, his reality was not a harmonious one. Being whole did not mean feeling orderly. 'Unity engendering dissension, that's the law of laws,' he mused.[5] The *grand homme* never completely identified with the grandeur he craved: his outlook on life was too sensitive to contrasts and spontaneous change. 'You feel frail and fierce, you are small and great . . . Everything comes and goes.'[6] Intrepid but at the same time self-aware, he was as accustomed to defeat as he was to triumph.

The dramatic episodes of Hugo's literary and political career – whether the victorious 'battle' against tradition that he led in French theatre in 1830 or his abortive rebellion against Louis-Napoleon's 1851 coup – were matched in their fervour by those of his private life, not least his passionate romances and his many personal tragedies. Born into a rapidly fluctuating society with increasingly estranged parents, he endured uncertainty and much loss. His anxieties of loneliness and feelings of exclusion were exacerbated by his fear of the mental illness that struck two members of his family. Each time his self-image fractured, new fault lines opened that he explored and attempted to repair. The mending process was neither smooth nor lasting in its effects.

No biopic has yet attempted to dramatize the entirety of this story, but Hugo's lengthy and eventful life is not the only challenge of scale facing those who want to know more about him.[7] Anyone who has read *Les Misérables* knows that it is a marathon read at nearly 1,500 pages; his other internationally recognized novel, *Notre-Dame de Paris* from 1831 (sometimes translated as *The Hunchback of Notre-Dame*), is no swift read either, at well over five hundred pages. These books are only two tests of the reader's stamina across a vast terrain. Hugo's inquisitive and imaginative character showed little restraint once he started writing.

The vastness of Hugo's complete works is intimidating when itemized: over twenty volumes of poetry; a dozen plays (the number increases to well over twenty if we include works written in his teenage years and those published posthumously); nine works of fiction (eight novels and one short story); multiple collections of non-literary writing including six books of essays (addressing history, literature and philosophy), three volumes of his political texts and speeches, and another two-volume edition of his notebooks; at least four editions of correspondence; three collections of travel writing; one opera libretto (for Louise Bertin's 1836 adaptation of *Notre-Dame de Paris*, *La Esmeralda*); and several thousand drawings and visual compositions, including a collection of seven hundred pieces held at the Maison de Victor Hugo museum in Paris.

The adaptations of Hugo's works make this landscape all the more sprawling. His fiction and drama have been the subject of scores of film and television adaptations worldwide, and of well over a hundred musical versions, including Verdi's operas *Ernani* (1844) and *Rigoletto* (1851), and the mega-musical known affectionately as *Les Miz*. The numbers are trickier to quantify when the net is cast beyond these media to other forms that Hugo's work has taken, such as print (including graphic novels and unofficial sequels), radio (there are at least ten recorded dramatizations of *Les Misérables* alone), song settings of his verse, and digital content online (where umpteen adaptations of Hugo can be found as fan fiction, videos and games).[8] Hugo's detractors may question whether he merits the label 'great' as a sign of literary quality, but the adjective's suitability for the range and mass of his work is indisputable.

Given these staggering dimensions, biographies of Hugo tend to have one thing in common beside their subject: they are nearly all dense, door-stopping books that demand (and, for the most part, reward) patient reading. One of the most recent is the largest. Even with the final instalment still to come, the first two volumes of Jean-Marc Hovasse's excellent French biography from 2001 and 2008 are greater in length (over 2,600 pages) than Hubert Juin's triptych (1980–86) and Max Gallo's two-volume study (2001), also both in French. Numerous single-volume works are available in French and English, but these are also mostly weighty studies.[9] In contrast, both Sophie Grossiord's illustrated 1998 biography and Marieke Stein's 2007 work hover around the 150-page mark, but these rare exceptions are only available in French and are written with a French audience in mind, most of whom will have learned something about Hugo at school.

These books are of course not much help to the many readers worldwide who do not speak or read Hugo's language (or to those

French readers looking for a less Francocentric take on him). Non-Francophone readers are limited in their options, especially since frustratingly many of Hugo's works have not been translated into English.[10] The last English biography is over twenty years old and more than seven hundred pages long. Graham Robb's 1997 work is sharp in its insights and extensive in its coverage, but its heft calls for a substantial investment of time. Furthermore, it of course does not reflect on Hugo's fortunes thus far in the twenty-first century, including the valuable new research that has been undertaken by literary scholars and historians.

Following on from these publications, my biography of Hugo offers a concise but full account of his artistry and activism in the light of what was, by any measure, a momentous life. His personal experiences are as indicative as his prolific works of how he understood everyday reality using a poetic imagination. I have written this book primarily for those readers who would like to know more about him and to have that knowledge available in a relatively succinct format. Readers who are already familiar with Hugo should also enjoy rediscovering his life story and his literary style while encountering new ways of thinking about him. Where possible, I have referred to existing English translations of Hugo's work so that readers can look further into the references I make. For the most part, however, the translations used in this book are mine and are taken from French sources. My priority in these instances has been to try to reproduce the pulse of Hugo's language with its blend of dexterity, intimacy and muscularity.

The 'Ocean Man'

No biography of Hugo can be conclusive or exhaustive, but his chosen metaphor of the ocean to describe his massive body of work has been important to how I have structured this book.

'The ocean alone is proportional to the magnitude, polymorphism, and permanence of Hugo's oeuvre,' as the organizers of the French National Library's exhibition 'Victor Hugo, l'homme océan' argued as part of the celebrations for the 2002 bicentenary of Hugo's birth.[11] There are distinct advantages in visualizing Hugo's work as an ocean of shifting surfaces and immeasurable depths that only imagination could fathom, and that only the winds of democratic change could help to sustain. The image of vast and endless fluidity evokes Hugo's mind working like the rhythms of the low and high tides. It signals that any reading must respect his emphatic contrasts and apparent inconsistencies as part of the whole, similar to the way unsettled waves and a dead calm can take over the same waters.

As a Romantic, Hugo felt the weight of a universe that he believed was boundless and forever on the move, marked by the constant passing of time and by nature's uninterrupted cycles of birth and death, of daybreak and nightfall. He saw such ostensible opposites as kindred, not contradictory: 'an opposite does not discount its counterpart; far from that, they complete one another.'[12] When one chapter ends, another begins. Supposedly discontinuous and discrete phenomena form part of the same motion, like the peaks and troughs of a wave. They need to be viewed not as being mutually exclusive, but as necessarily complementary and, in this sense, interchangeable.

This flux bore the trace of a divine life force that was ultimately liberating in its dissolving effect on human history and the human heart, neither of which could be unchanging or seemly in such a world as ours. Hugo aligned that liberty not only with his own creativity but also with the modern society that was developing in his lifetime. In his eyes, his imagination had to be as free and uninhibited as nature. He could then understand life's changeability and probe its mysterious design, lending both social relevance and spiritual weight to his ideas.

Victor Hugo, *My Destiny*, 1857, pen and brown ink wash, gouache. As the eye scans from left to right and the crashing wave grows larger, the focus of Hugo's 'destiny' falls not on the ship's struggles but on the mounting swirl of the ocean itself.

Modelling himself as a conduit for the variability he perceived around and inside himself, he toyed with the idea of using the word 'ocean' as the heading for a preface to his complete works in 1846:

> the whole oeuvre is an immense horizon of glimpsed ideas, works I began, and of sketches of plans with not entirely clear outlines . . . a swirling together of drifting works into which my mind throws itself without knowing if it will re-emerge.[13]

He had earlier likened the age of modern literature to a vibrant ocean, suggesting a personal fascination that became more prevalent during his exile when he was surrounded by the English Channel on the islands of Jersey and then Guernsey.

It was there that he coined the term *homme océan* or 'ocean man' to describe artistic genius as the channelling of nature's free flow into civilization. Criticizing his childhood naivety, he no longer believed that the poet had to change the direction of history, like Hercules turning the course of the River Alpheus, since 'the flow should not be turned – it has to be channelled'.[14] He concurrently used the symbol of a continuous but not always direct course to naturalize the development of his ideas. He claimed to have moved from conservatism to republicanism 'as you would pass from a river into the ocean'.[15] Open horizons and the dynamism of nature made poetic and political sense to him. They gave his mind a convenient pretext for embarking into unknown and strange waters as a fanciful but certainly not frivolous thinker.

The oceanic comparison can also be thought through in less abstract and more practical terms for the purposes of this biography. Hugo's self-described equivalence with an ocean means that his huge expanse of work cannot simply be pumped into a single critical overview. Draining his ocean entirely in this way would require numerous large volumes that even Hugo's most avid fans would have difficulty wading through. Nor would taking a small number of discrete samples from that ocean suffice, since this would risk isolating those individual parts from the whole and bringing its overall agility to a halt. Instead, a selective but consistently illustrative approach will highlight the key patterns at work by looking at Hugo both up close and more broadly.

This approach is analogous to the interplay in Hugo's writing between the particular and the general. He identified individual components to examine – such as personal encounters, real and fictional human figures, or chosen moments in history – but related their character to the broader sweep of time and to 'the great anxiety of what might be' in his search for meaning.[16] A similarly versatile approach when reading Hugo enables his ocean's varied movements to be observed, along with the cyclical forces driving those tides. Each phase of his life and each medium he used to express himself will be addressed so that his diversity and complexity become clear.

Hugo's desire to hold everything together in a comprehensive vision was quickened by a life of private and public discord. Hostility between his parents and then heartache in his own marriage and extramarital affairs; animosity between the rival artistic tastes of nineteenth-century France; enmity across the country's political spectrum and between France and its European neighbours; the period's growing gulf between political life and spiritual faith – there was certainly no lack of opposites for him to try and reconcile. His determination to settle that unease was obstructed, however, by those competing elements he encountered both in his life and within himself.

His need to become an instrument of reconciliation ran deep thanks to a poetic mind that was always attentive to the inconsistency of human emotions. 'Inside us a sombre sight is offered: a serpent is visible at the water's source, and mistrust crawls deep within our souls.'[17] It is no coincidence that Charles Baudelaire, the wordsmith of modernity who dedicated three of the poems in *The Flowers of Evil* (1857) to Hugo, claimed the entitlement to self-contradiction as one of the rights of man.[18] Hugo was the arch Romantic, courting harmony but always obliged to live with dissonance, who made a virtue of that necessity by envisaging it as a way of living a fuller life and moving closer to God.

As a result, my biography of Hugo will consider a man of contrasts: an individual of reasonable build and height but with a vitality that led friends to describe his physique as one 'which could have earned him a living as an artist's model' and 'almost Herculean';[19] a celebrity with a sociable manner and an infectious laugh, but who disliked parties and excessive drinking; a devoted family man and consummate saver who did not recklessly spend or gamble, but whose ardour for the comforts he found in the opposite sex manifested itself in a series of affairs that often exhibited the compulsions (and remorse) of an addict; a believer who was never baptized and who never attended Mass, but who had a pantheistic faith in God and the idea of universal love, and who peered beyond the grave during spiritualist seances in Jersey; a politician with more interest in ethical principles and generalization than in shrewd politicking; and a writer whose abhorrence of violence and desire for unity did not subdue his attraction to the ruinous forces at work in history and nature. A figure comes to light that is more modest and apprehensive than a victorious or self-obsessed demigod. This is the reality of a life and mind driven by conviction but vulnerable to collapse, whose appetite for grandeur and gratification was matched by his aching sense of disenchantment and limitation. To look at Hugo in these ways is to see a more engaging, more human subject than cliché permits, and to take a deeper, more 'Hugolian' perspective.

This book's chapters divide Hugo's life into five chronological parts, followed by a discussion of his public funeral and his iconic afterlife. A brief conclusion at the end spotlights Hugo's ability to unsettle received wisdom about the social ideals that he and his work are so often called upon to endorse. That disruptive potential is important to keeping him relevant in the twenty-first century by ensuring that his often-challenging voice is not muted by slick sound bites. Consequently, this conclusion reiterates my biography's central concern: that both Hugo and his work need to be read on their own terms, rather than solely in hindsight and from a distance.

1

'I want to be Chateaubriand or nothing' (1802–22)

Scribbled down on 10 July 1816, Hugo's oft-cited desire to 'be Chateaubriand or nothing' has become shorthand for his ambition. Today, Chateaubriand is more familiar as a type of steak than as the name of a writer, but Hugo was not foreseeing the times when he would often be figuratively butchered by his critics. Instead, his eyes were fixed on prestige. In early nineteenth-century France, François-René de Chateaubriand was the idol of many young minds searching to make sense of a world whose social and religious foundations had seriously faltered. He ushered in the first wave of French Romanticism with his innovative writing style and his rejection of the materialist thinking of the Enlightenment, which he believed had facilitated the violence of the Revolution and the deaths of many fellow aristocrats. Hugo was not alone in his admiration: Lord Byron, Hector Berlioz and Alfred de Musset were also deeply affected by what Chateaubriand called the *vague des passions* (the vagaries or fluctuations of passion) and the emotional indeterminism that it disclosed.

Although Hugo's statement seems like a prophecy of future greatness, it should be read merely as an example of a fourteen-year-old boy's youthful exuberance rather than as the visionary confidence of a mage in the making. His childhood and adolescence can easily be seen to predict what was to come, given his precocious talent and early successes. Nevertheless, his early years reveal how winding and trying that path would be. Those contortions and challenges explain the attraction to Chateaubriand as much as any teenage dream of fame. Having fled France in 1791 as a royalist émigré and travelled the New World, Chateaubriand's eventual reintegration and growing criticism of the Revolution and Napoleon set an example in Hugo's mind of the lengths to which a writer should go when voicing ideas. But more than the moral example, Chateaubriand epitomized the Romantic sensibility that would appeal to Hugo as a way of lending meaning to his own fluctuating experiences.

When casting his eyes back over his youth, this flux was a tide that Hugo tried to bring to order. In the opening poem to his 1831 book *Autumn Leaves*, entitled 'This Century was Two Years Old', the poet presents himself as the product of two implicitly opposed sources: Breton blood from the maternal side of his family in the Vendée department of western France, and paternal ancestors to the east in Lorraine. 'I know where I come from,' he says, faithful to the mix of blood coursing through his veins, passed down from 'my father, the old soldier, my mother, the Vendéenne!' The absence of a verb to express any action in this last line ends the poem with a rather immobile image. It feels at odds in its stasis with a portrait that has briefly glossed the 'pulsing waves' ridden by the poet thus far in his life.

As would become Hugo's habit, he was attempting to reconcile himself with a fractious past, described here as the 'stormy breath' of imperial conquest under Napoleon. 'How this high destiny of glory and terror . . . in every wind blowing made my childhood drift,' he recounts, before reassuring his reader of his poetic powers to remain afloat, as fuelled by 'my head, a furnace where my spirit catches fire'. Yet the attempt to emphasize his ability to chart these waters ends anticlimactically. The closing inertia is made more conspicuous by the lack of any conjunction to join the final line's two parts, suggesting an ambiguous relationship to the memory of his parents' marriage and its union of opposite bearings on the national compass. With an ideologically progressive but politically conservative mother, and with a bellicose but decorated military father, Hugo was exposed to a divisive family life that mirrored France's own discord as the country forged sweeping and confrontational paths towards its post-Revolutionary future. The integration of his ambivalent roots into a natural poetic evolution was never going to be easy, although the emotions it released and his feelings of affinity towards Chateaubriand began helping his imagination to work with contrasts rather than simply against them.

1802–15: The Baby of the Family

Fate had apparently decreed that Hugo would be born well equipped to meet these challenges. As his father told him when he was nineteen, Hugo had been conceived on one of the highest peaks in the Vosges Mountains. He knew his father well enough to understand that he was prone to highly subjective claims, but Hugo himself was not opposed to relying on the imagination in order to shed light on the truth. It was little wonder to him that he could have wide-ranging perspectives as a poet when his creation had taken place so close to the heavens above.

Victor-Marie Hugo was born on 26 February 1802 in the eastern French town of Besançon. His birth had been difficult for his 29-year-old mother, Sophie Trébuchet. He was a frail and pallid baby, with a large head on a weak neck and frame. It was feared that he had been born with rickets and that he would not survive. His father, a 28-year-old army commander called Joseph Léopold Sigisbert Hugo, waited for several days to let friends know of his third son's arrival, until his prospects looked brighter. Even at birth, Hugo was veering towards death and being pulled between incompatible fixtures.

'This Century was Two Years Old' underscored the debt that he owed his mother for her physical and emotional nourishment, but in reality the infant did not enjoy Sophie's undivided attention for long. By the summer, he and his older brothers Abel (born in 1798) and Eugène (born in 1800) had relocated to Marseille. A few months later, their mother travelled to Paris to procure the help of family contacts in resolving some awkward friction between her husband and one of his superiors. Whether it was during this period that Sophie became intimate with her youngest son's godfather, General Victor Lahorie, is open to speculation. In the interim, Hugo and his brothers moved first to Corsica and then to Elba in the Tuscan Archipelago, where Léopold's battalion had been posted. Léopold fretted over his parenting skills in letters to his wife.

Only six years into their marriage, the two were quickly becoming estranged. Hugo's portrayal of them leads readers to believe that this distance was fated to open up, given Sophie's royalist sympathies and Léopold's republican loyalties. But this crisp antithesis masked a messier attraction between the exuberant Léopold and the more poised Sophie. Both shared an interest in Enlightenment philosophy, and libertarian ideals encouraged neither to hold back with their desires. By the end of 1803, Sophie had taken her three army brats back with her to Paris. With her help, Lahorie was lying low in the city after participating in a conspiracy against the first consul, Napoleon Bonaparte, who was about to reorganize his realm into the First French Empire to stave off the threat of a royalist restoration. Sophie's Voltairean views allowed her sons to enjoy an open-minded and secular upbringing, but she was not in any rush to update their father, who complained of receiving only infrequent news from her.

In contrast to his marriage, Major Hugo's career was going from strength to strength, although his progress might have been swifter had his family not been associated with Lahorie. Napoleon had his sights set on the Kingdom of Naples, where Léopold took his men in early 1806. Before the year was out, Léopold had captured the famed Neapolitan resistance leader Fra Diavolo, which helped lead to his promotion to colonel and marshal in a kingdom that was now ruled by one of his strongest supporters, Joseph Bonaparte (Napoleon's older brother). The next winter, Sophie decided to join him in Italy, tempted by the security that her husband's new rank could offer the family. Léopold, however, had begun living with an Englishwoman called Catherine Thomas.

Hugo was now old enough to form conscious if sporadic memories, especially of Rome and its baroque grandeur. The journey to Italy opened his eyes not only to the delight of discovering new cultures but also to the reality of conflict both in Napoleonic Europe and closer to home. The French Empire used gruesome tactics to deter resistance to their occupation: nailing human bodies to trees or displaying severed heads at the roadside was not uncommon. Not directly associating their father with this landscape, Abel, Eugène and Victor were excited to see him again and marvelled at his uniform, but the family reunion was short-lived. Citing how busy he was, Léopold quickly directed his family to Naples. He was no longer capable of living with his wife. His efficiency in suppressing opposition was needed in Spain following the Madrid uprisings of May 1808, where Joseph Bonaparte now ruled, so he – and Catherine – left Italy that summer. Sophie and her sons held out until the end of the year, then made their way back to Paris via Milan. Letters exchanged with her husband displayed a growing animosity.

The return to Paris in early February 1809 greatly offset whatever disquiet Hugo was feeling as the son of a frustrated mother and a distant father. Sophie, still receiving considerable financial support from her husband, soon found a new property to rent with an overgrown garden near the Latin Quarter. It was here, after the family's sixth move, that Hugo first experienced a stable home life. Like his brothers, he had been worn out by the repeated displacements and sometimes quietly cried alone without anyone knowing why.[1] Their time living in the spacious ground floor apartment of the old Feuillantines convent was a world apart from what they had previously known. The garden provided an ideal play area for his brothers and the children of Pierre Foucher and his wife, who were family friends and neighbours. It also instilled within young Victor a deep appreciation of natural beauty. Thirty years later, he would celebrate the 'fair but alas too brief childhood' spent at the Feuillantines.[2] His poem imagined the garden begging Sophie to leave him to the natural teachings offered by the rustling of the trees, the scent of the flowers and the sight of the evening sky. 'Sparing me from boring prisons,' he adds, 'she entrusts my young soul to their tender lessons.'

This Edenic education was enhanced by two other 'masters' he singled out for praise in this poem: 'an old priest, and my mother'. The former was a man called de la Rivière who worked at the nearby primary school. In consultation with Sophie, he taught Latin to Eugène and Victor and introduced them to Tacitus and Homer, in addition to encouraging some competition through translation exercises.[3] Sophie had already brought along her two youngest sons' reading skills by making frequent use of a local *cabinet de lecture* (a public reading room). Missing from this poem's acknowledgements was the man whom Sophie was hiding in the crumbling chapel at the bottom of the garden. Under the name of 'Monsieur de Courlandais', Lahorie complemented the liberal education that Sophie's sons received. He ate dinner with the family and helped the boys with their homework, showing a particular interest in the Roman Republic and in ideas of democracy.

The novelist who created the idyllic garden at the Rue Plumet in *Les Misérables*, and whose plots often involved atypical reconfigurations of families, undoubtedly owed much to the Feuillantines. Moreover, the Romantic for whom ideas and ink would always win out over artillery and bloodshed, and the rebel who would chastise an empire, can be glimpsed during this eighteen-month awakening, nurtured by the pleasures of learning and by the garden's vibrancy in an environment that was far removed from his father's military lifestyle. It came to an end in December 1810, when Lahorie was arrested after being lured out of hiding by the new minister of police. Sophie sensed that this was an opportune moment in which to make herself scarce.

The family began their journey to Spain in March 1811. Eugène and Victor insisted that they sit on the two exterior seats of their carriage for the best view. Studious and determined, the youngest Hugo had become a competitive child and did not want to miss out on this new adventure. As in Italy, the escape to a foreign land broadened but also darkened his horizons. During a month's stop in Bayonne on the southwest French coast close to the Spanish border, he claimed to have seen René-Charles Guilbert de Pixérécourt's melodrama *The Ruins of Babylon* several times, whose apricot-coloured riders and Arabs covered in chain mail exposed him to the thrill of popular theatre like never before.[4] It was also here that 'his virility declared itself' when he saw the chest of the landlady's daughter as she read stories to him, demonstrating how easily the sounds of words and the body's senses could work together.[5]

Having been obliged to wait for an escorted convoy, the family experienced a similar delay once they reached Valladolid as reinforcements were needed before they could progress any further. More outings to the theatre helped to pass the time. These interruptions were Sophie and her sons' first taste of the reality that Léopold was facing. Having continued to garner favour and become General Hugo, he had been tasked with governing the province of Ávila in central Spain. Resistance fighters could be hanged on display on the road from Valladolid to Madrid before their severed heads were nailed above local church doors. What was already a tricky road to travel due to its various geographical perils was made more nerve-wracking by such macabre encounters.

The convoy finally reached Madrid in June. The family was shown to the palace of the former ambassador to France, the luxury of which stimulated Hugo's interest in decor.

His father was less than ecstatic when he learned of Sophie's arrival while away in the Guadalajara province. The rupture that had been delayed in Naples was now inevitable in Madrid. Léopold filed a petition for divorce and had their three sons sent to a seminary college. The tutelage of the pious priests was a far cry from the teaching style they had been used to and did not warm them to the Church, even though they were able to attend preparations for bull runs and the city festival of San Isidro. In swift response to her husband's actions, Sophie stressed her innocence to Joseph Bonaparte, whose goal of stabilizing his new kingdom through the appearance of decorum made him a sympathetic arbitrator. The task facing King Joseph became tougher in October, however, when Léopold learned about Lahorie's arrest, piquing his suspicions about his wife's behaviour. Léopold had returned to Madrid as the king requested, but cut off financial support to his wife while his sons continued to suffer the double blow of being intellectually incarcerated and physically separated from their mother. The animosity persisted into the new year, although Joseph's interventions eventually persuaded both sides to reach an agreement: Abel would stay in Spain as a royal page, and Sophie would return with Eugène and Victor to Paris in the spring, receiving a pension that Joseph had created using some of Léopold's budget to cover her needs.

The family separated. To add further distress, Hugo saw two grisly sights on the journey home: a condemned man led to the scaffold in Burgos, and a rebel's still bloody corpse at Vitoria, maimed on a cross. Back in the Feuillantines, Abel's initial absence until late 1813 would not be the only alteration to how life had been before Spain. Lahorie continued to oppose Napoleon's rule and was executed in October 1812 after a failed coup (which may well have involved Sophie). Hugo only learned his name afterwards, if his memories are to be believed, thanks to his mother. Later the following year, the Hugos were forced to leave the Feuillantines due to urban planning by the Paris authorities and moved to the ground floor of a property in Paris's sixth arrondissement. There, they were again close to Pierre Foucher and his family, who had recently moved, and had a garden. Sophie's sons began composing their earliest poems with her full approval. Sophie, for her part, found that her mourning for Lahorie was soothed when the Russian and Prussian armies reached Paris in late March 1814, bringing Napoleon's rule to an end. As a loyal soldier of France, Léopold found himself serving the new king, Louis XVIII.

While Europe took tentative steps towards peace, Hugo's parents were involved in acrimonious divorce proceedings. Léopold gave his half-sister, Marguerite Martin, power of attorney in his battle against the woman he referred to as *la démon*, with instructions to sell the household goods and take custody of his two youngest sons. Even though they barely knew their aunt, Eugène and Victor were taken to her home in nearby Saint-Germain-des-Prés in June. Their brotherly bond became increasingly important as their parents' marriage became ever more strained. Hugo had already tried his hand at writing two theatrical works in 1812: a burlesque comedy called *Hell on Earth* and a fairy-tale melodrama, *The Devil's Castle*. Having enjoyed the puppetry shows in the Luxembourg Gardens, he and Eugène were now improvising plays for puppet theatre together in a mutual escape.

1815–22: Towards Adulthood

It was Pierre Foucher's turn to try and arbitrate between the Hugos, but he only managed to get Léopold to replace the divorce plea with an official separation on his terms. In January 1815 the court ruled in

General Hugo's favour. An especially unpleasant face-to-face confrontation followed in which Léopold's burst of verbal and physical aggression towards his wife was witnessed by several friends and domestic staff, giving Sophie some legal advantage in securing a small pension.

For the next three and a half years, Eugène and Victor were residents of the Pension Cordier, a boarding school near the Abbey of Saint-Germain-des-Prés in which their thirst for autonomy and their disappointment in their father grew more intense. Shut up in attic rooms that were uncomfortably hot during the summer and freezing during the winter, the two teenagers had no holidays, no permission to go out alone and only limited visitation rights. During Napoleon's short-lived return to power in the period known as the Hundred Days in spring 1815, Léopold left for Thionville to fight the Prussians in a valiant defence of the northeastern border. Back in Paris, his sons waged a campaign of their own by throwing themselves into their studies. Among other activities, they routinely learned, then translated, Latin verse and wrote several dramatic works to be performed in school. His imagination seemingly receptive to the family hostility, Victor also began imagining the end of the world in poetic verse, writing an apocalyptic ode entitled 'Last Day on Earth' and a redemptive epic called 'The Deluge' when he was fourteen.

It was in the summer of 1816 that Hugo wagered his future on becoming Chateaubriand. His objective smacked of his father's conquering verve in its tone, but its ultimate goal showed that he identified far more with his mother. Chateaubriand was a Breton aristocrat who had opposed the Republic and an emotionally literate writer who preferred the powers of the imagination to those of the musket. In short, he personified and validated Sophie's differences from General Hugo as the young Victor Hugo saw them during the early years of the Bourbon Restoration, and in Lahorie's absence he provided another role model that was more suited to the aspiring poet's needs than his reticent father. Chateaubriand's novellas *Atala* (1801) and *René* (1802) used a luxuriant, rhythmic prose to capture both nature's vibrancy and the heart's surging impulses, neither of which fitted with the measured tempo of ordered reason. In the same vein, he published *The Genius of Christianity* (1802), which argued that the Enlightenment had misunderstood God and had consequently thrown France off course rather than directed the country towards true progress. Christianity's contributions to civilization and to the arts had been vital, he claimed, in acknowledging all creation as divine. Such an argument asserted that there was more to the world than meets the eye, and that the cruelties of time and mortality had greater creative purpose than the Enlightenment's secular bent could measure.

For Hugo, as one of his later odes hinted, Chateaubriand also showed him how to envisage individual sorrow not as a descent into despair but as a learning curve towards a greater self-understanding. The harsher the climate, the more heroic the vessel:

> Chateaubriand is one of those glorious ships
> That desire the hurricane more than the zephyr.
> ... We see you, after each fall from on high,
> Descend yet higher still than you had climbed before.[6]

This spiritual view of suffering as transient allowed Hugo to ennoble the adversity that he, his brothers and 'my dear mama'[7] were dealing with at the hands of his father's chosen emissary, their aunt Marguerite. 'Madame Martin' was a sore point in letters jointly written by Victor and Eugène to their father. Her habitual slander of their behaviour made it easier to preserve some filial warmth and undoubtedly emboldened Hugo to take the stance of moral indignation that would later define so many of his political interventions. 'Your letter proves to us that our conduct is being maligned,' he and Eugène wrote to their father, 'and that – whatever we do – people will always know how to incriminate us in your ear. No matter.'

To Léopold's mind, their requests to go out on free days or for everyday items like new shoes were all motivated by his estranged wife, as was their apparent disrespect towards their aunt's authority. Believing that Sophie had passed on her ingratitude to their sons, he dismissed their case for better treatment, and in the process failed to conceal his resentment. The anguish in their letters is palpable: 'it is extremely painful for us to see you treat our mother so wretchedly.'[8] When Abel later stepped in as an intermediary, Léopold felt slighted by what he described as impertinence. He was too embittered to recognize that his eldest son, like his two others, was offering him a scapegoat in Marguerite for his own austere choices. If a Bonaparte had been unable to broker peace between the Hugos, it was unlikely that a seventeen-year-old would have had more luck.

Imitating his hero, Hugo used these troubles to concentrate his mind rather than let it become disinclined. In the second half of 1816, having devoured Voltaire's tragedies, he focused his energies on writing a verse tragedy of just over 1,500 lines. In this play, the Egyptian throne has been usurped by the tyrannical Cambyse, so one of the king's royal guards, Irtamène, fights to restore the crown to the rightful monarch and save his own wife at the same time. The romance of an expressive and royalist hero saving an innocent spouse and defeating a usurper and his regime allowed Hugo to imagine an idealized denouement to his own circumstances. On a more objective level, the play's structure indicated that he had the creative stamina to utilize the twelve-syllable metre of the French alexandrine, as wielded by giants of seventeenth-century French theatre such as Molière and Jean Racine. It also showed that he understood the conventions of French Neoclassical tragedy, as codified by Nicolas Boileau in his canonical *L'Art poétique* (1674), even if it betrayed some impatience with those rules, including the unity of space. He had been learning more about the genre in philosophy classes with Eugène at the prestigious Lycée Louis-le-Grand as part of their schooling, where theatre formed an important aspect of the school community.

Hugo proudly offered *Irtamène* to his mother as a New Year's gift for 1817. Sophie was not the only one to have noticed his burgeoning talents. A young schoolmaster called Félix Biscarrat, who would become a supportive friend, submitted a poem that Hugo had written to the Académie française's annual poetry competition. This ode to the pleasures of reading was noted by the judges, who were amazed that it had been written by a fifteen-year-old fan of Virgil. Abel used his connections in Paris's literary circles that summer to spread the news of his brother's fine debut, not least to their father. His little brother, meanwhile, dedicated the coming term to writing two more dramas: a revenge tragedy, *Athélie, or the Scandinavians*, whose northern setting recalled Voltaire's attempts to revitalize the French stage by looking beyond classical or biblical locales; and a comic opera, *Chance is Good for Something*, which ignored the Neoclassical expectations of verisimilitude in favour of indulging the imagination's fancies. This second work was Sophie's New Year gift for 1818, proving that his mother was the first audience he had in mind.

The die was soon cast for a career as a writer. Sophie won custody of her sons and an increase in allowance. After their graduation from school they began living with her again in modest lodgings in the heart of Paris's Left Bank. Abel had turned away from a military career now that the Restoration had taken hold, and beginning in July he held monthly gatherings of his literary contacts in a local restaurant, to which both of his brothers were also invited. Eugène and Victor enrolled on law courses in November, but this was a cover for their father's benefit so that they could continue to experiment with their true interests. The group was predominantly formed of conservative royalists, or *ultras*, echoing Sophie's political opinions.

In 1819, Hugo published two of his poems individually, the first of which he dedicated to Chateaubriand, and entered another ode into the annual competition of France's oldest academy, the Académie des Jeux floraux. Odes were considered an old-fashioned and supercilious form that had inspired the first poets, but Hugo was convinced they allowed the venting of more impassioned and relatable feeling. So as not to offend contemporary sensibilities that expected the self-discipline of Neoclassicism, the boisterous and strong-willed content of his odes was sufficiently policed by the structural conventions that he had mastered: lengthy, complicated stanzas in which any variance of metre and line length would be patterned rather than unpredictable. His prize-winning entry memorialized the re-erection of Henri IV's statue on the Pont-Neuf as the first monarch of the House of Bourbon. Hugo had attended the procession and ceremony with his mother and brothers the previous year. 'To the sage's roused eye', thought Hugo, the incorrupt spirit of sovereigns like Henri IV will survive whatever violence befalls such monuments. The statue's return was therefore cause for national pride: 'Make no mistake, this august image's aspect / Will lessen our ills and sweeten our happiness.'[9] Having espoused the virtues of timeless symbols, Hugo chose a trophy over the cash prize as his reward.

His mounting success encouraged him to found a new periodical with his brothers called *Le Conservateur littéraire* (The Literary Conservative), which was an allusion to Chateaubriand's political review, *Le Conservateur*. It first appeared in December and would be distributed twice a month for just over a year. During this run, Hugo would write more than all the other contributors combined, producing well over a hundred poems, translations and critical essays. These articles, which marked his first steps into journalism, included attacks on the post-Revolutionary atheism that he, like Chateaubriand, believed was stifling the French cultural imagination, although his respect for Voltaire acted as something of a buffer to the full-throated Christian royalism of *René*'s author. Notably, his priority was to ensure the future stature of French letters, so the starting points of his arguments were literary and aesthetic in nature. Reflecting on contemporary theatre, and adopting a nostalgic air that made him seem older, he regretted that 'people no longer ask if a poet is of the right school, but if he's from the right party'.[10] He was able to value the energetic dialogue and spectacular staging of Casimir Delavigne's historical tragedy *The Sicilian Vespers* (1819) without following the trend in the Restoration press to deride or glorify its author's liberal politics.

Artistic merit might have been his preliminary concern, but Hugo displayed little of the political inexperience of a parvenu. Early in 1820, he published his ode 'The Death of the Duc de Berry', shortly after the king's nephew had been assassinated by a Bonapartist. He captured the sentiments of grief-stricken royalist salons across Paris and procured a financial reward from the royal family itself. This achievement prompted Chateaubriand to invite the city's newest prodigy to meet him. Proving that there may be some truth to the adage that fans should avoid meeting their heroes, the meetings with Chateaubriand were a disappointment. Hugo found him aloof to the point of being condescending. The first encounter was so underwhelming that Sophie had to persuade her son to accept the invitation to return the following morning, when the reserved 52-year-old became more accessible as he took a bath in front of his young guest. Hugo would maintain respectful contact with him and pay further homage in his odes, but the spell had been broken. If Chateaubriand could not fulfil the ideal of literary genius, then Hugo realized he would have to do it himself.

His drive to meet this goal was fortified by more than professional ambition. Back in 1818, he and Eugène had started to accompany their mother on her regular visits to see the Fouchers. These soirées were oddly quiet affairs: Pierre would read while his wife, daughter

Adèle and Sophie busied themselves with sewing; Hugo, Eugène and Victor Foucher would sit around the central table with little to do. In Hugo's case, the hushed atmosphere made his thoughts all the louder as he looked at Adèle, with whom he used to play at the Feuillantines. Now fifteen, she had abundant dark hair and large eyes. The following April, they both escaped the usual routine and declared their love for one another in the garden. By 1820, they were signing off their correspondence as 'your faithful wife' and 'your husband'. Both promised themselves to one another. When Adèle's parents found out, they were uneasy about their daughter being courted by a poet with no steady source of income and so they consulted Sophie. Less than thrilled at the news, Sophie angrily told her youngest child that a general's son did not marry an office clerk's daughter. It was a double shock for Hugo: he was forbidden to see Adèle again, and in his eyes his mother was no longer the victim of an unfeeling authoritarian parent but had become one herself.

Hugo's literary and domestic fates were now entwined. Success as a writer would grant him more leverage to make good on his intentions to marry Adèle. He recommitted both to his work and to the practicalities of self-publicity. He noted that this schedule left him no time in which to keep up to date with his other correspondence, much to the chagrin of his friends,[11] but he used his work to impel his strength of will:

> Glory is the end I desire . . .
> For the eaglet, born of squalls,
> Only atop the clouds' dark palls
> May his flight soar up to the sun.[12]

In the first July edition of *Le Conservateur littéraire*, he published a mournful poem, 'The Young Outcast', knowing that the Fouchers subscribed. 'I loved you without delusion, and I love you with a fury!', the poet Raymond laments to his lost love Emma, before beseeching her to burn these verses so that no future lover will be able to call her purity into doubt. In the autumn, he declined Chateaubriand's offer to work alongside him in his ambassadorship to Berlin, fixated on his chosen career rather than on a political apprenticeship. He again measured the royalist pulse with an ode celebrating the birth of the Duc de Berry's posthumous son, which he followed up with another ode for the baptism of 'the miracle child' in May 1821. That same month, his mother's health worsened. Sophie had been unwell, with problems with her chest and nervous system, and had incurred sizeable costs for her care. On 27 June, at the age of 49, she died with her sons by her side. They were forced to sell her few remaining objects of value, including some watches and silver, to pay for her funeral.

This 'immense, irreparable loss' left Hugo and his brothers 'devastated with sadness',[13] but the grief enabled not one but two different reconciliations. Hugo wrote to his father to let him know the news and reminded him that his mother had always insisted that he and his brothers be respectful towards him. He was an accomplished general, after all. With one parent gone, Hugo was more hopeful than ever that he could find some rapprochement 'because he will be a father to us for as long as he wants to be'.[14] He also needed his father's financial backing as he launched his career. The money was not as forthcoming as he might have liked, leaving him with the kind of hardship that he would recreate for Marius's student days in Les Misérables. But with Sophie gone, Léopold was less suspicious of his sons. Within weeks, he had given Hugo his permission to marry Adèle, provided that he secure a stable source of income as a husband. He also announced that he would be marrying his mistress Catherine.

More immediately, Sophie's death removed a major obstacle to Hugo's romance with Adèle. The two lovers had been writing to one another in secret, partly because Hugo believed that his mother would have eventually consented to their engagement. In mid-July, the Fouchers headed to Dreux, 72 kilometres (45 mi.) west of Paris, to put some distance between their daughter and her grieving paramour in case anything rash should happen. Unable to afford the coach fare, an undeterred Hugo left on foot to pursue them. The trip resulted in the earliest of his pieces of travel writing in a letter he sent to Alfred de Vigny, which was full of Romantic abandon as he described his fascination with the ruins of Dreux castle. He managed to persuade Pierre Foucher of his honourable intentions. Foucher, like General Hugo, would only consent to their union if the budding poet could earn enough to support a future family.

Hugo's love for Adèle, which had yet to be consummated, had been building for over two years, and he had been challenged by not one but two fathers to prove himself. It was all the motivation that any self-respecting poet needed. By September the following year, he had been awarded a royal pension, which combined with his projected annual earnings would give him an income that would be well in excess of 2,000 francs per year. The pension came thanks to the success of his *Odes and Assorted Poems*, which he had published in June with Abel's help. This compilation of odes old and new had been influenced by Alphonse de Lamartine's hugely popular *Poetic Meditations* (1820), which had been reissued in January with an additional two poems. Lamartine did for poetry what Chateaubriand had done for prose. He heralded a new Romantic vogue by rejecting the Neoclassical interest in timeless and ordered truths and instead subjecting the lyric self to the fluidity of time and to the deeply temperamental nature of human emotions.

Hugo's collection could not boast a standout piece like Lamartine's superlatively melancholic 'The Lake', but the short preface gave him his first opportunity to draw his work together and to sound out his methods. He had two reasons for writing the book, literary and political, but he stressed that 'the latter is the consequence of the former'. Two fundamental ideas followed: poetry's limitless scope,

Jean Alaux, *Victor Hugo*, 1825: one of the earliest portraits of Hugo.

and the recognition that beneath reality lay another way of being 'which shows itself, resplendent, to the eyes of those whose solemn meditations have become accustomed to seeing in things more than the things themselves'. 'Poetry', therefore, 'is all that is intimate in everything'.[15] For all his conservatism, Hugo was making a plea for the autonomous poet as the only truly sighted artist.

The preface's mystical overtones resonated with the Romantic Catholic revival that Chateaubriand had helped to spur. It married the Revolution's libertarian principles with Christian beliefs in

Julie Duvidal de Montferrier, *Portrait of Adèle Foucher* [Adèle Hugo], *c.* 1820, oil on canvas.

humanity's dual status as both mortal and immortal. Hugo's friendship with the Breton abbot Félicité Lamennais was formative in this respect, especially given the parallels in their later attraction to social liberalism, which they would share with Romantics like

Lamartine. Lamennais had been a regular contributor to *Le Conservateur littéraire*, having found a wide audience for his 1817 *Essay on Indifference in Matters of Religion*. He offered Hugo a more inquisitive approach to spiritual faith than Sophie had. He was also essential to Hugo's wedding plans as he certified that Hugo had been baptized in Italy, even though such a ceremony had never taken place. This would not be the last time that Hugo would rely on deception in the name of love.

On 12 October 1822, Victor Hugo and Adèle Foucher were finally married at the church of Saint-Sulpice in Paris, followed by a reception at the War Ministry where Pierre Foucher worked. In his later years, Hugo claimed that he and his wife made love no less than nine times on their wedding night, which became a founding myth in his reputation for virility.[16] This excessive (and quite possibly exaggerated) sexual performance was perhaps to be expected, given his restless nights alone, but it also suggested a compensatory behaviour and pointed to more unruly feelings beyond purely runaway joy. During the wedding festivities, Eugène became exceptionally agitated and had to be helped by his brothers. Foreshadowed for several years by odd and volatile behaviour, Eugène's breakdown had been brought on by a conflation of unbearable pressures: his mother's death; his father's remarriage; and his growing jealousy of his younger brother, whose literary achievements surpassed his own and whose new wife he had quietly desired for himself.

This turn of events shattered Hugo, although he was thankful that their mother had not lived to see her middle child admitted to an asylum. Within two years, doctors determined that Eugène's mind was beyond repair and the family should not visit him. This withdrawal of visitation rights stood until his death in 1837. Eugène's illness no doubt motivated his brother to try to make the most of the blessings he enjoyed as 1822 ended. Hugo had married his childhood sweetheart and announced himself as one of France's most promising new writers. But his mother's death had deepened his dread of loss and his brother's schizophrenia spurred apprehension about the unstable line separating the self-control of genius from the infirmity of madness. As much as Hugo's adolescence had driven his desires to become the premier writer of his time, they had also fed his fears of the darker side to his teenage ambition. What if he failed and was, ultimately, worth nothing?

Worries that Hugo raised with his father about Eugène, and feelings he expressed to Adèle during their courtship, confirm that these anxieties were deeply rooted in his sense of self. He feared that 'the tools society uses to treat the [mentally] ill, captivity and inactivity, might simply feed a melancholy whose only cure, it seems to me, would be free movement and distraction'.[17] He admitted that this solution was almost impossible to realize, but the energy he exhibited throughout his life was surely primed by this belief in the need to keep both mind and body occupied. His letters to Adèle display a related but separate need, as revealed through the avidity of young love: that of validation from his loved ones. 'It would be impossible for me to live without being loved by you,' he told her. Fearing both abandonment and indignity, he warned her that he could be desperately jealous. 'Love is neither true nor pure if it is not jealous in nature.' He was envious of her younger brother for sometimes sharing her bed and of her uncle for enjoying an evening out with her. Such envy might explain why Adèle maintained a cool composure and why she observed that she had difficulty understanding poetry. Hugo had hoped his responses would reassure her that 'the most unaware person can feel poetry': 'Poetry is the soul, what they call my talent is nothing other than my soul.'[18] In baring that soul for a living, its hungers and ailments would necessarily become more apparent as he entered young adulthood.

2

'I am a force in motion!' (1823–35)

The likening of Hugo to an irresistible force on the move – 'une force qui va', to quote his play *Hernani* (1830) – is commonplace to describe his energetic ascent towards celebrity between the early 1820s and the mid-1830s. Not simply a brash declaration, this saying divulges a vacillating, even feverish spirit. At a midpoint in the play, the hero Hernani pleads with Doña Sol, the woman he loves, to live without him and accept her imposed marriage to her uncle, Don Ruy Gomez, rather than end her life:

> You think me perhaps
> A man like all the others, a being who is
> Discerning, who straight to his dream's desire will run.
> Do not fool yourself! I am a force in motion!
> Blind and deaf, an agent of woeful formlessness!
> A soul of misery fashioned out of darkness!
> Where do I go? I know not. But I feel driven
> By a whirlwind murmur, a senseless intention.[1]

As a Hugolian archetype, Hernani's fate is not preordained by the gods, as in classical tragedy, but by a turbulent way of being that is ingrained into his character. A nobleman by descent but born an outcast in exile from sixteenth-century Spain, the young bandit rallies against the authority of a king whose father killed his own. He is motivated by love for his father, who stands as a symbol of

Castilian honour, and for Doña Sol, who embodies the purity of love itself, but he does not see his life moving forward along a stable path. He defines himself as restless rather than steadfast, subject to the same disquiet as Hugo, which is conveyed in part by the verse's enjambment (whereby single lines run onto the next and are not end-stopped). Neither his vision nor his hearing orient him, but he is aware of something impulsive and indeterminate within that pushes him into the future.

In isolation, Hernani's claim to be 'une force qui va' could be seen to imply a positively buoyant and resolute self-understanding. In the context of the full speech, however, such vigour is qualified as a searching and at times ungovernable wave. Hugo explored this mutable sense of self more and more as an abiding truth. The goals he had set himself quickly came into reach as his daily reality transformed: the teenager courting his true love became the husband fathering a family; the general's son imagining acclaim became the garlanded commander-in-chief of a new artistic vogue; and the would-be Chateaubriand investing in the truth-giving powers of literature became the Romantic who eagerly questioned the point of poetic vision. Other changes that he had not envisaged would accompany these shifts, which he would need to integrate somehow into his self-image: public conflicts; his gradual move away from his mother's royalism; and marital strife, which recalled memories of his parents' troubled marriage. Each of these developments occurred as the French crown forcibly transferred from the House of Bourbon to the House of Orléans, obliging the new monarchy to rely on a revolution to take the throne while asserting its own historical legitimacy to secure power.

These metamorphoses enhanced Hugo's instincts from his adolescence that today's meanings and tomorrow's promises would always be far from clear or stable. 'A poor eulogy for a man if they say that his opinion has not changed in 40 years,' he wrote in his journal: 'for that man, there was neither any day-to-day living, nor thoughtful application of his mind to the facts.'[2] Finding the right means of articulating and investigating this kind of flexible thinking became essential and generated the first of two major periods of literary productivity in his career in which he wrote some of his best-known works. First respecting but then questioning the social conservatism of the day, he launched a volley of successes on both page and stage. He affirmed his right to artistic innovation while asking venerable questions about the nature of history and humanity.

His efforts also convinced him that the two most precious assets he could have were 'a conscience at ease and total independence'.[3] Only these two attributes could retain their worth, he thought, in a world whose values seemed open to negotiation. His mind's artillery had to fight for them above all else as he tried to defend his writing from becoming a matter of routine while finding some coherence in who he was. He would discover that some strands of his world, no matter how hard he tried, were destined to remain awkwardly knotted rather than woven neatly together.

1823–7: Preparing the Ground

Hugo's love for Adèle poured into his verse: 'It is you whose look makes my sombre night brighter,' he gushed.[4] They welcomed their first child, named Léopold in honour of General Hugo, in July 1823. The baby's health was poor, however, and less than three months later he died. In an ode he wrote to the late Revolutionary heroine Marie-Maurille de Sombreuil while his frail son was still alive, Hugo begged God, 'Do not take back those given life by your light.'[5] In another poem composed shortly after Léopold's death, he visualized a radiant afterlife immersed in a 'torrent of love', but this blissful picture is tinged with self-reproach:

Oh! In that august world where nothing is fleeting,
In these streams of happiness free from gall and bile,
Child! Far from your mother's face smiling and weeping,
Are you not an orphan on high?[6]

As the final stanza of a single-sentence ode, the poet's cumulative tribute to God's benevolence buckles under its own weight and exposes his torment. The tacit guilt that Hugo could not be a father to his son darkened his joy at having become a parent, bringing bliss and distress into a mutually reinforcing association in his mind at just 21 years old. Léopold is the least well known of Hugo's children, but his death was significant in that it was the third loss of a loved one in as many years, following Sophie's death and Eugène's breakdown, and it made the start to married life bittersweet. 'To a Child's Shadow' drafts a literary blueprint for Hugo's labours of grief: an attempt to register the despondency of death for those still living while at the same time probing that emptiness for any signs of consolation. Crucially, neither sensation could be allowed to cancel out the other lest the emotional sweep would be lost.

Professionally, at least, his career was progressing. The poet Émile Deschamps launched *La Muse française* in the summer of 1823, giving Hugo a new if short-lived platform. The first edition featured his review of Walter Scott's recently published novel *Quentin Durward*. Hugo saw an opportunity to hasten his climb towards literary fame by studying how Scott's historical fiction had rejuvenated the past. Where Lamennais reminded modern society of its need for a deep connection with the world, Scott attended to that need from a less spiritual angle by encouraging a closer human relationship with history. The massive popularity of *Waverley* (1814) and the series that followed had given rise to 'Scott Mania' in French bookstores, theatres and even fashion trends. Hugo had already experimented with fiction in *Hans of Iceland*, which he had published earlier that year. A mix of medieval quest, gothic horror and melodrama, the novel told the story of two young lovers in seventeenth-century Norway, whose romance intersects with political intrigues and social unrest. Several of his emerging interests came to the fore, such as injustice, the relationship between freedom and revolt, and the monstrosity of human nature, as memorably embodied by the bloodthirsty dwarf of the title. But it was more of an eager first step than a stunning debut. Its playful narrator was more interested in parodying the excesses of his assortment of genres than in humanizing his characters.

Scott's work offered the novice an attractive apprenticeship in modern prose epics, finding in history an intimacy not dissimilar to that which Hugo had spoken of in his 1822 *Odes* preface. He applauded the way Scott brought history alive and how he created new prospects for a literary form that had previously been dominated by the sentimental and gothic genres. 'No novelist has hidden more instruction within more charm,' Hugo claimed.[7] Scott proved that fiction could do more than quench thirsts for tawdry stories of emotionalism and violence, without having to sacrifice the rousing potential of its descriptive powers. His novels saw history's purview through human emotions and individual experiences, observing how lives are shaped by the contingencies of time and place. Fiction fostered a consciousness of history that could keep up with the velocity of social change and not lose sight of the past's diversity. The essay on Scott set a high benchmark for fiction, but it also raised the stakes further in an early instance of Hugo's common rhetorical method: identify a record of excellence, then propose how it might be steered towards a yet brighter future and insert himself into that line as a natural successor. He felt that Scott had not gone as far as he could have done with the possibilities afforded by historical fiction, although 'he has at least opened up the way forward'.[8] Where exactly that path would lead remained unclear.

The literary disagreements of the 1820s provided the necessary environment in which to draft more substantial ideas. These squabbles involved the Classicists, who were wedded to notions of *style noble* and *bienséance* ('nobility of style' and 'propriety'), and the Romantics, who favoured a less regulated means of self-expression. Romanticism gained traction in France later than in Britain or Germany due to the country's codified Neoclassical traditions, as enforced by the Académie française. The word 'romantic' was originally a derogatory adjective in the seventeenth century, used in relation to the fantastical nature of medieval romances (so called because they were written in the romance languages that had descended from Vulgar rather than Classical Latin). By the late eighteenth century, however, it had taken on a more positive use to describe natural gardens and landscapes. These associations with informality allowed 'romantic' to become the watchword for the opposition to Neoclassicism. They alluded to natural flourish and uninhibited creation in place of Neoclassicism's universalized and unchanging morality.

Hugo initially did not want to be drawn into the hostilities, prefacing a new edition of his *Odes* in early 1824 with his refusal to take sides. He urged his fellow poets to follow in the footsteps of Homer, Virgil, Dante and Milton and light society's way forward, instead of lighting fuses and brandishing the divisive banners of Classicism and Romanticism. Given that the first wave of Romanticism in France had risen at the turn of the century with Germaine de Staël, Benjamin Constant and, of course, Chateaubriand, his discreteness can seem odd. He did not share their aristocratic background, but his objectives bore more than a passing resemblance to their beliefs. These writers feared that post-Revolutionary France would suffer the fate of ancient Rome and be overrun by corruption, disorder and tyranny. They argued that French culture needed to look away from the ancient world's classical precepts of coherence and uniformity and turn instead to the teachings offered by Christian and medieval thinking, which celebrated divine mystery, natural wonder and aesthetic delight.

French literary and artistic forms needed to expand in order to accommodate emotion and subjectivity, and to reflect the country's individuality in its specific historical contexts. In so doing, French culture had an obligation to enlighten the country both intellectually and spiritually in order to prevent public opinion from being manipulated by base instincts.

With a childhood of parental and military conflicts behind him, Hugo's reticence is understandable. He also had a family to think of, with Adèle pregnant for the second time. The challenge for Hugo and other contributors to *La Muse française* was how to facilitate France's spiritual evolution in ways that would be intellectually and morally palatable in the wake of 1789's Declaration of the Rights of Man and of the Citizen. The Congress of Vienna (1814–15) had either strengthened or restored the pre-Napoleonic monarchies of Europe, but the continent's appetite for the French Revolution's principles of self-determination was becoming more apparent, as were the shortcomings of various crowns to recognize these rights. These tensions had been signalled by a succession of uprisings in 1820 in Spain, Portugal and Italy, and were exacerbated by the subsequent Greek War of Independence against the Ottoman Empire.

It was in that conflict that Lord Byron died in the spring of 1824 while fighting alongside the Greeks. Byron instantly became a martyr for a disillusioned generation who perceived the Constitution of 1814 as heaping power into older hands through the French Charter's bill of rights. Hugo mourned 'the noble poet' in a judicious essay that used the word 'romantic' only once, but in a response he published several weeks later to claims that he was a Romantic at heart, his momentary use of the pronoun 'we' betrayed where his sympathies really lay.[9] Those sympathies looked unsafe in April 1825 when both he and Lamartine were awarded the Legion of Honour and invited to the coronation of Charles x, who had become king after his brother Louis xviii's death. But as Charles veered towards reactionary conservatism, Hugo's doubts grew, especially as Chateaubriand had been hounded out of the Ministry of Foreign Affairs and General Hugo himself had been refused the Legion of Honour. His thawing relationship with his father had made him more receptive to the general's politics at a crucial moment.

Hugo had also become friends with Charles Nodier, who held weekly gatherings at the Bibliothèque de l'Arsenal in Paris where he was librarian. The older Nodier shared with Hugo his passion for one of Romanticism's demiurges, Shakespeare, whose tragi-comic plays were being rehabilitated in France after generations of antagonism towards his impulsive mixing of classical genres. Nodier also accompanied Hugo to Charles x's coronation in Reims, after which their party travelled along the Franco-Swiss border to Lyon. Nodier's historical knowledge brought the local landmarks alive, reminding Hugo of the significance of preserving the past and learning from it. Most importantly, his Sunday salons at the Arsenal began drawing together writers, artists, journalists and philosophers, including like-minded poets such as Lamartine, Vigny and the Deschamps brothers. These salons provided Hugo with a new forum in which to test his ideas and to generate support for his work. The assertive spirit of the Vendée that he ascribed to his mother and the battle acumen he associated with his father were about to become weaponized.

As 1826 dawned, Hugo set about consolidating older works to clarify in his own mind where he was heading. He started by revising a short story that he had written in 1820, *Bug-Jargal*, into a novel. Its focus on the Haitian slave revolt of 1791 was timely: the former French colony of Saint-Domingue had been recognized as the independent nation of Haiti several months earlier. The story is narrated by a young army captain, Léopold d'Auverney, who recounts to his infantry how he was saved during the rebellion by a slave, Pierrot. Pierrot is really Bug-Jargal, a descendant of African royalty. He condemns the violence of the other rebel slave leaders, as personified by the spiteful Biassou, and ultimately gives his life to save those of his men.

It would be easy to stereotype this novel, either as a revolutionary plea for racial tolerance that was astoundingly liberal for its time, or as a facile recycling of colonialist tropes that idealized the noble savage figure and conversely demeaned the violent slave hordes. Both readings are oversimplifications of a novel whose complexities reflect Hugo's attempts to work through his personal evolution using his imagination. The anti-Revolutionary standpoints of the Restoration are not difficult to find in the stark contrast between Biassou's cruelty, which stirs hatred by appropriating the rhetoric of 1789, and Bug-Jargal's nobility, which often translates into pacifism. 'Will our cause be more holy and more just,' he puts to Biassou, 'once we have exterminated women, slit the throats of children, tortured old men, burned colonists in their houses?'[10] But the oppression of the slaves reveals violence and despotism to be systemic within social order as much as radically opposed to it. The slaves suffer under d'Auverney's malicious aristocratic uncle, but they are also shown to be bewitched by Biassou's scheming and by the calculated superstitions of his *obi* or priest, Habibrah. The novel's racial politics are similarly unsteady. Bug-Jargal's moral and physical strength exoticizes the black male body, and the narrative voice is perplexed, if not repulsed, by slave customs. Yet the novel holds its black hero in an esteem that surpasses that of its white narrator, who takes more time to figure out what is happening than the reader, and whose storytelling abilities are gently ridiculed by his men.

Such esteem suggests that Hugo identified as much with the wronged outcast as he did with the privileged insider. The fraternal bond between Bug-Jargal and d'Auverney implies a desire for romanticized heroes whose humanity sets them apart from the wickedness or ignorance of others, irrespective of race. Furthermore, the fact that both heroes are in love with the same woman, and that both will be dead by the final page, summons Eugène's memory and exposes an anxiety that the only conclusive solution to the novel's domestic and political conflicts is death. This ambiguity and concerns over the novel's verisimilitude left the critics dissatisfied, and the book today still huddles in the shadow of Hugo's later fiction. Thematically and structurally, however, *Bug-Jargal* showed that Hugo had found in narrative a potent means of self-expression: the authorial voice that felt no need to be authoritative or self-certain in what it was saying.

The autonomy and authenticity that he desired for his work was explicit in his new edition of his odes, entitled *Odes and Ballads*, in which he reached beyond the alexandrine and experimented with the breezier octosyllabic and heptasyllabic metres of Renaissance poetry. The alexandrine's heft still served him well in a new ode to Lamartine ('Torrents of poetry burst forth out of your breast!'),[11] but the quicker pace of poems like 'Timbalier's Fiancée' allowed for more capricious moments. In a new preface, Hugo distinguished between odes as being soulful and ballads as fanciful. Whereas the loftier ode's eloquence brought a classical wisdom to the events witnessed by the poet, the ballad was a more whimsical lyric, recalling the medieval troubadours and the popular oral tradition. Neither was anathema to the other, provided the artist was concerned more with the world's inherent flux than with the regularity of convention. Nodding to Romanticism's derivation as a term, Hugo qualified this freedom as the natural order of a New World forest rather than the disciplined gardens at the Palace of Versailles. The argument's political ramifications were not lost on him: 'In literature, as in politics, order is wonderfully congruent with liberty and is even its consequence.'[12] He persisted in refusing the title of Romantic, but his logic relied more on his unease with fixed definitions than it did with what Romanticism stood for.

It was in 1827 that Hugo's status as the voice of a new generation became deafeningly obvious. Feeling stifled in his conservative royalist garb, he swapped this regalia for something less ill-fitting. His ode 'To the Vendôme Column' in February was published in the *Journal des débats*, which had grown suspicious of Charles x's intentions towards the French Constitution. The poem was a swift response to the controversy that had been sparked when, during a reception for the Austrian ambassador, four of Napoleon's marshals had been announced without their imperial titles. Like many children of the Empire, Hugo took the insult to be both national and personal. Importantly, it enabled him to rationalize his early conservatism (and that of his country) as the first steps of a broader fruition rather than his defining origin. He spoke of the pride that the column at Paris's Place Vendôme instilled as a monument to Napoleon's historic victory at Austerlitz, and of his outrage that foreign powers would malign French honour. The final stanza called upon his 'brothers' to salute their lineage: 'We have all grown up by the tent, at the camp's lines.'[13] The Napoleonic adventure was over, but these 'eaglets banished from the skies' could still fight for their country using the lyre rather than the sword. The ode's tone of filial praise and its pugnacious stance towards the European monarchies confirmed that he understood his generation's frustrations and its ambitions for greater sovereignty.

His move in April to the rue Notre-Dame-des-Champs in Paris's sixth arrondissement gave his growing family a garden, now that he and Adèle had a nearly three-year-old daughter, Léopoldine, and a five-month-old son, Charles, but it also provided his entourage with a new meeting place. That autumn, the Romantic Cénacle was born in gatherings organized by Hugo and the critic Charles Augustin Sainte-Beuve, whom Hugo had sought out following his commendatory review of *Odes and Ballads*. Over the next three years, this coterie's young participants included writers such as Honoré de Balzac, siblings Armand and Louise Bertin (whose father ran the *Journal des débats*), Alexandre Dumas, Théophile Gautier,

Alfred de Musset and Gérard de Nerval, and artists like Eugène Delacroix and the Devéria brothers, as well as the sculptor David d'Angers. It was a formidable battalion.

The Cénacle's rallying cry came in a new essay from Hugo that would become one of his most important critical works. The previous summer, he had begun writing a play about Oliver Cromwell. As a regicide who drew on popular support for political legitimacy, *Cromwell* represented an allegory for France's post-Revolutionary history, but the play's bloated size (four times the length of Racine's *Phèdre*) made it impractical to perform and continued Hugo's run of misfortune with the stage. Five years earlier, his melodrama *Inez de Castro* had been accepted at the Panorama-Dramatique, only for the theatre to close before production began, and his collaborative attempts to adapt Scott's *Kenilworth* (1821) had gone unfinished. Hugo cut his losses and published *Cromwell* with a lengthy preface at the end of 1827. The play's failure to be performed was quickly mitigated by its introduction's popularity as a demand for artistic self-determination, supported by Sainte-Beuve's articles in *Le Globe*. According to Gautier, it struck the Cénacle like the passing of the Ten Commandments.[14]

To be sure, the preface to *Cromwell* was neither as singular nor as spontaneous in its conception as the Tablets of Stone. The critique of Neoclassical tastes for symmetry and correctness had been under way since the eighteenth century, not least thanks to the *Sturm und Drang* ('Storm and Stress') movement in German literature and music. Coming after Stendhal's 1823 pamphlet *Racine and Shakespeare*, Hugo was assaulting an already prone target, but his opportunism and conviction set his preface apart. Shaking the pen rather than rattling the sabre, he argued that the Romantic era's spirit of free expression could not be solidified into a mould or template. The point was to poeticize art, not to theorize it: 'We are not building a system here.'[15] Nature's perpetual creativity was to be the only model, which had to be both reflected and probed in the artwork by turning the artist's mind into a *miroir de concentration*, a focusing or concave mirror. Neither 'obsolete classicism' nor 'false romanticism' could give the artist the necessarily wide field of vision or intensity of insight.

What was needed was not a new set of rules, but the freedom to work without limitations, 'with permission not from Aristotle but from history'.[16] The theatre should mimic and scout life's natural flux rather than freeze those movements into some eternal moral order. The unremitting span of human experience could not be voiced by a sanitized and supposedly noble register alone, any more than it could be codified on stage into the Aristotelian unities of time, action and place (determining that there is a single action unfolding in a single space within one given day). Life was too dramatic to be structured into distinct components, which Hugo grouped around the poles of the sublime and the grotesque.

Art had to abandon Neoclassicism's moral and aesthetic hierarchies and embrace how these opposites interacted organically with one another. 'True poetry, whole poetry, lies in the harmony of contrasts . . . Everything comes together yet pulls apart, as in reality.'[17] This dramatic quality was at the heart of Christianity for Hugo. Christian theology revealed the 'double basis' of existence through the body's impermanence and the soul's immortality. It had been best espoused by writers who troubled rather than stiffened the divisions between opposites, such as damnation and redemption (poets like Dante and Milton), humdrum reality and playful fantasy (storytellers like Rabelais and Cervantes) and the tragic and the comic (especially Shakespeare). These writers had challenged the customary privileging of the lofty over the lowly to offer a more authentic understanding of what it meant to be part of creation.

The preface's indifference towards hierarchies of value had direct social implications as well, linked with the benign image of Shakespearean theatre bringing together a national community during the Elizabethan period. If the sublime and the grotesque were permeable and interchangeable, if the ugly could be beautiful and vice versa, then high culture and populist entertainment need not be diametrically opposed, and the two-tier theatrical culture of old need not stand. The established genres of tragedy, comedy and opera, and the popular modes of melodrama, vaudeville and fairy tale, could infuse one another to allow for more versatile works and less segregated audiences. The goal was not to preach to the audience, as was often the case with the moralizing tendencies of melodrama, nor to offer the edifying resolutions of classical drama, but to offer a wide-ranging experience that could energize rather than prescribe the audience's thoughts and feelings. 'Art gives us wings, not crutches.'[18]

1828–31: Victory

Audience tastes were not quite ready for what Hugo's ideas meant in practice. His adaptation of *Kenilworth* was performed in February 1828 as *Amy Robsart*, with costumes designed by Delacroix, and introduced his signatures as a playwright: the role of human passion in the absence of divine providence; the attention to local colour and historical detail through ambitious staging; and the inversion of moral values away from their usual social moorings, seen in the potential grace of those from low birth and the nobility's capacity for base sentiments. Nevertheless, the play's treatment of the comically grotesque actor Flibbertigibbet (his friskiest name for a character yet) as a courageous figure, along with its retention of the heroine's murder from the novel, proved too much in a play that was excessively long, especially as the previous three French adaptations had all softened Scott's tragic denouement.

Achille Devéria, *Victor Hugo*, 1829. Achille and his younger brother Eugène Devéria were both part of Hugo's Romantic Cénacle in the late 1820s.

The start of 1828 had been difficult. General Hugo's death the previous month left 'an immense and profound void'.[19] When handling his father's estate, he would find Léopold's correspondence with Sophie, including letters pertaining to her infidelity. Discouraged from the stage and in mourning, it was in poetry and in fiction that Hugo reasserted himself. The general's loss enabled a psychological break of sorts with his youth, as suggested by another edition of *Odes and Ballads* in which he presented his definitive poems thus far. Over the next year, Hugo explored his imagination's latitude while continuing to ponder how best to be a poet in the modern age.

Les Orientales, or *Orientalia*, underscored his reluctance that art should have some pragmatic message to impart. Byron's verse had popularized the image of a Romantic, middle-eastern Orient, and his death had invigorated support for Greek independence, but Hugo's preface announced *Orientalia* as a 'needless book of pure poetry'. Hawkish readers need not have concentrated their gaze too strenuously had they ignored this warning: Hugo's swipe at Boileau's *L'Art poétique* and favourable comparison of the 'tiger' Ali Pasha[20] with the 'lion' Napoleon betrayed some discernible purpose in resisting the values of the current French regime (borne out by the poem 'Him' in praise of Bonaparte). Yet these references formed part of a more artistic motivation. 'The poet has no account to settle,' Hugo stressed. 'He lets you loose in this great garden of poetry, where there is no forbidden fruit,' and where he wandered freely among the nomadic peoples, exotic landscapes and heated rebellions.

Orientalia proved that Hugo had advanced beyond appropriating classical forms. His poetic virtuosity dazzled his readership with its visual richness, fantastical journeys and musical effects. The collection reflected the Romantic trend for the Middle East to be used as a stimulus for a non-representational approach, in which art stepped outside the figurative space of recognizable forms and became more self-sufficient. Hugo's picturesque powers of suggestion, not demonstration, enabled a less reasoned, more instinctive experience. He embarked on a sensory voyage that apprehended meaning through more than just the optical and the literal. He enlarged his poetic range through a vocabulary of unfamiliar words, like the myriad vessels of 'Navarino' such as barcaroles (from Venice) and caravels (from Portugal), and through inventive structures that often mixed their metres and employed the circular character of refrains.

Orientalia's most famous poem is one of its most illustrative pieces. In 'The Djinns', the poet's abode is visited in the dead of night by a swarm of djinns (supernatural creatures from Islamic mythology). Over fifteen rhyming stanzas, the poem's metre progressively builds from duosyllabic beats to the decasyllabic lines at its midpoint before scaling back down again. The visual and aural effect allows the reader a more unmediated access to the besieged poet than description alone: just as the fire-breathing djinns spread across the night before abandoning the skies, words pervade and then evacuate the page as the sounds accumulate and then scatter. Stillness ('Walls, town/ And port') gives way to terror ('Dragons and vampires fill the sky!') before silence reigns ('I note:/ Each flees'). It is the verse equivalent of a roller coaster, dizzying the reader's senses for no reason other than its creator's whims.

The poems appeared in January 1829, one month before *The Last Day of a Condemned Man*. Unlike *Orientalia*, this short novel, in which a nameless man recounts his final hours before his execution, did have a more overt purpose, although one that was still dependent on literature's ability to elicit feeling rather than deal in formulaic or rudimentary terms. The novel cemented Hugo's reputation as one of France's most vociferous opponents of capital punishment, and was cited a century and a half later by Robert Badinter, the French minister of justice who oversaw the death penalty's abolition in 1981.

The Last Day focuses on the condemned narrator's humanity rather than on questions of guilt, as he never proclaims to be innocent. Consequently, the novel's humanitarian concerns cannot be divorced from its literary interests in how best to represent the despair of the narrator's tortured consciousness. This is why Dostoyevsky remembered the novel just after enduring the horror of a mock execution in late 1849, and why parallels have been drawn with Albert Camus' *The Stranger* (1942).[21] The condemned man's anonymity and his first-person narration at once universalize and personalize his plight in 'a diary of my suffering, hour by hour, minute by minute'.[22] The claustrophobic severity of his bewilderment is conveyed through the novel's structure, at just under one hundred pages in length but with nearly fifty brisk chapters, and through its crisp prose, which allow no respite from the narrator's physical and mental convulsions. The unforgiving conditions of prison life and the hyena-like crowd waiting for the execution are described with the same detail as the man's nightmarish hallucinations of decapitated heads and a dark abyss awaiting him after death. *The Last Day* was as much psychological drama as it was political statement, the alienation of which hinted at the ominous darkness that could shroud Hugo's own mind.

These two achievements in verse and prose brought Hugo much acclaim, but he knew that he needed similar success in the theatre if he was to lead the literary culture of the day. He had to lay claim to what had been the hallowed ground of French letters since the Golden Age of Louis xiv. When Dumas became the first Romantic to stage his work at the famed Comédie-Française in February 1829 with his prose drama *Henri iii*, Hugo knew he had to move swiftly. He wrote *A Duel Under Richelieu* as a verse drama to modernize the Neoclassical five-act formula. The play followed the plight of a courtly heroine trying to obtain mercy for her two lovers, who had defied the royal ban on duelling. It delighted the Cénacle and Baron Taylor, the director of the Comédie-Française who had feared losing audiences if the theatre did not move with the times. Taylor secured the rights, but Charles x's censor banned the play due to the portrayal of Louis xiii as a weak monarch whose power had been overtaken by that of his chief minister, Cardinal Richelieu. The minister of the interior tried to placate an indignant Hugo with a tripling of his annual pension, but Hugo refused to accept this. Mocking the current king through his ancestor had never been the intention. Once Sainte-Beuve spread the story in the press, Hugo looked ever more like his generation's frontman: someone whom conventional thinking wanted to restrain, but whose principles could not be compromised.

With the moral tenacity he had developed in his teenage years now on public display, Hugo quickly refocused and wrote *Hernani*. It was accepted at the Comédie-Française for a February debut featuring one of French theatre's biggest stars, Mademoiselle Mars. The Spanish theme echoed Pierre Corneille's seventeenth-century tragedy *Le Cid*, which had partly defied the classical unities, and protected Hugo from any critics worried about slurs on French history. He was fearful that the regular *claque* (professional applauders used by theatres) could not be depended upon in what was still a bastion of tradition, so he replaced them with supporters organized by the Cénacle, many of whom dressed eccentrically for the premiere as a sign of their non-conformity.

On 25 February 1830, these young Romantics collided with the Classicists in a rowdy melee of catcalls, litter-throwing and physical scuffles. The *bataille d'Hernani* would be repeatedly fought over the coming months. Although fairly conventional in its plot of doomed young lovers, *Hernani* was a deliberate provocation against Neoclassicism. Structurally, the play showed no unity of place or time: moving from Saragossa to the Aragon mountains to Aix-la-Chapelle, the action took place over several months. At the visual and spatial levels, Hugo dismissed Neoclassical anxieties towards spectacle in a vibrant *mise en scène* that intensified the drama on stage rather than distracted from it. The actors wore sumptuous costumes designed by the painter Louis Boulanger to exhibit the local colour of the settings. In rehearsals, Hugo had instructed them to ignore the more measured movements of classical training by exploiting Pierre-Luc-Charles Ciceri's lavish set design to the full and by venting more passion through this freedom of movement.

Most offensive of all was Hugo's rejection of the *style noble*. He wrote like a poet rather than a versifier, with free feeling and no sense of prudishness, and with the willingness to unsettle both the usual ordered rhythms of French verse and the pretentious tone of monarchic regimes. The play's opening lines deployed the disapproved technique of enjambment to allow for less stilted dialogue. The second scene in Act One typified the play's insistence upon new dramaturgical standards. The farcical sight of King Don Carlos hiding in a cupboard and his vulgar line, 'Dammit, I'm leaving!' were unbecoming of a monarch but in keeping with his characterization. After Hernani and Doña Sol had died together in a tragic denouement, it mattered little to the more exhilarated members of the audience that the hero's suicide had been dependent simply on a promise he had made to his lover's fiancé. Plot verisimilitude was secondary to the characters' emotional credibility. Critics mostly denounced *Hernani* as silly and conceited, but ticket sales were strong and allowed Hugo to clear his debts by the summer. 'The classical cabal wanted to bite,' he reflected, 'but thanks to our friends it broke its teeth against *Hernani*.'[23]

The desire for greater freedom that *Hernani* had invoked would soon be apparent on the streets. In mid-March, 221 deputies passed a vote of no confidence in the intransigent Charles x and sparked a period of unease that resulted in the Three Glorious Days of the July Revolution. Hugo believed that Charles and his government got what they deserved for their failure to adapt.[24] The July Monarchy began under Louis-Philippe, the Duc d'Orléans. A cousin of Charles who supported monarchical reform, Louis-Philippe admired the British constitutional monarchy and wanted to follow a *juste milieu*, or middle way, between absolutism and democracy. In practice, this would mean that only the very wealthiest middle-class citizens would have a say in elections and government under the 'Bourgeois Monarch'.

Having taken over two years since the preface to *Cromwell* to have a theatrical hit, Hugo knew that revolutionary ideas needed time to mature before they could succeed. A more open

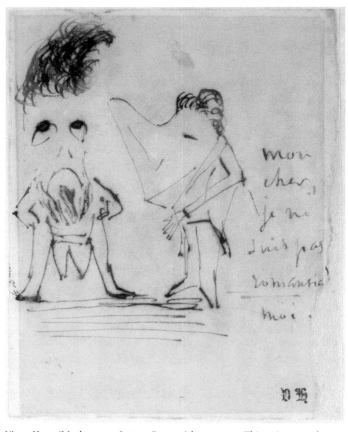

Victor Hugo, 'My dear man, I am no Romantic', *c.* 1830–40. This caricature pokes fun at the self-importance of the Classicists who had opposed the rise of Romantic art. Hugo would often draw such caricatures, especially to entertain his children.

constitutional monarchy seemed the surest steward to take France forward, so Hugo erred on the side of steady but not unchecked progress: 'One day we will have a republic,' he privately reckoned, 'but let's not pick in May the fruit that will only be ripe in August.'[25] His official response was to publish a poem in tribute to the July Revolutionaries, who had taken up the mantle of their forefathers: 'You are truly their sons! . . . You needed but three days to break from your tethers.'[26] It was an early sign that he was more open to the merits of collective force than the anti-Revolutionary royalist of his late teens. The metaphor of an erupting Vesuvius lent the revolutionary tide the feel of an unstoppable natural surge.

What had been less ebullient had been the writing of his next novel for the publisher Charles Gosselin. Hugo had been doggedly busy. One demand on his time was his home life: he now had two more children, Victor and Adèle. He was also perturbed by his banishment from Adèle senior's bed. After five pregnancies and nearly eight years of being married to the country's newest celebrity writer, an exhausted Adèle wanted distance. As Hugo came to understand through confessions from Sainte-Beuve over the next year, there was another reason for Adèle's coolness: she had become very close to his friend and the two had feelings for one another. Under pressure from his publisher and physically rejected by his wife, Hugo locked himself away to write the promised novel, which to Gosselin's relief was published the following March.

Notre-Dame de Paris made Hugo's name across Europe, mixing melodrama and medieval history against the backdrop of late fifteenth-century Paris. His longest novel yet gave his imagination greater range than his previous works of fiction, showcasing all the flair and pathos that had made *Hernani* so riveting. Taking his reader inside, around and atop Notre-Dame by drawing on his own experiences during his leisure time, he utilized multiple angles of vision and demonstrated his poetic sensitivity to mood through the play between light and darkness. It was an electrifying display, from more intimate scenes within darkened interiors to impassioned set pieces such the night-time battle outside Notre-Dame between the Royal Guard, the Parisian outcasts and the cathedral's hunchbacked bell-ringer, Quasimodo. This visual energy partly accounts for why the novel has been adapted nearly twenty times on screen, including the 1996 Walt Disney animated film.

Notre-Dame de Paris' themes are myriad in their coverage of human passions and social ills. Intent on developing fiction's philosophical and historical potential, Hugo encapsulated all these meanings in a single word. The narrator states that the novel is about one thing – *anankè*, or 'fate'. He claims in a brief foreword to have found this Greek word inscribed on a wall inside one of the cathedral's towers. For Notre-Dame's archdeacon, Claude Frollo, fatality is inescapable and must take its course, as he insists when he sees a fly caught in a spider's web. This world view of inevitability has both moral and social ramifications, coming as it does from a Catholic priest who is convinced of humanity's sinful nature, and at the end of the fifteenth-century reign of Louis xi, whom history remembers as the 'Universal Spider' due to his scheming wiles. However, in a novel where the captain of the King's Guard and the Church's main representative are shown to be morally fallible, and where the king's magistrate is both deaf and rancorous, the mechanisms of law and order are upended, along with any fixed arrangement of right and wrong. This questioning of certainties urges a more ambiguous reading of fate, as symbolized by the cobweb. The web has been niftily spun by the spider and, as Frollo himself summarizes, the fly was too focused on the sunlight to see the danger. Fate, in this respect, would still be a matter of interconnected forces as symbolized by this image, but it would be determined as much by individual desire as by uncontrollable circumstance.

These tensions between predestination and volition form the novel's dramatic basis. A beautiful young Roma girl called Esmeralda, who is a member of Paris's outcast community, finds her fate entwined with that of three different men. At the same time, those stitches are unpicked, since these figures' initial characterizations do not hold firm and their supposedly pre-set tracks are thrown off course. Esmeralda was not born a gypsy outsider and learns of her French heritage in a melodramatic unmasking of her past. The chivalrous Captain Phoebus reveals himself to be shallow, consciously playing on Esmeralda's teenage infatuation with him, while the pious Frollo harbours carnal desires and becomes agonizingly unhinged by his lust. Both men behave duplicitously and cause Esmeralda great harm. In contrast, Quasimodo seeks only to protect the bohemian after she shows him compassion during his public flogging for his attempted kidnap of her (which he had carried out under his master Frollo's orders).

Quasimodo is the grotesque proven sublime: a one-eyed man-monster who realizes that he need not be as inhuman as the gargoyles surrounding him. His Latin name, as a composite of 'as if' and 'mode', is a fitting sobriquet for someone who is seen as physically and morally only partial in his being, yet his physical deformities and social ostracization buttress the most tender and selfless of all the characters. His youth at just twenty years old infers wider horizons than he at first sees (and offers a wink to the Cénacle that their time was now). Esmeralda's sympathy for him frees up his awareness of his humanity, causing him to lament, 'Oh, why am I not of stone like you!' to the gargoyles as he begins to feel a gamut of emotions.[27] His courage and ingenuity in defending her within the cathedral's sanctuary, in addition to his despondency following the novel's tragic climax, redraw the conventional outlines of beauty and goodness. The impact upon the reader is such that many have taken Quasimodo to be the novel's main character. In 1833, Frederic Shoberl entitled his English translation *The Hunchback of Notre-Dame*, which has often been taken up in other translations and adaptations.

Hugo's original title and his dislike of the English version confirm that the real star for him was the medieval cathedral that Quasimodo calls home. The cathedral represented his generation's openness. Hugo's fascination was not religious, especially as Frollo's Catholic dogma is responsible for much of the misfortune that befalls the main characters. Notre-Dame concretized the *mélange des genres* from the preface to *Cromwell* and its goals to encompass a more inclusive idea of artistic and national identity. If Quasimodo is the human embodiment of Romantic sensibility, then Notre-Dame is the hunchback's architectural sibling who likewise challenges the concept of fate as something set in stone. Both share the indeterminate, unfinished character that Hugo saw as a prerequisite for creativity.

Notre-Dame could be considered ugly by aesthetic purists who would bemoan her hybridity of Romanesque and Gothic styles, or undesirable in the eyes of non-believers wanting to secularize the public domain. However, Hugo believed that the cathedral redefined beauty and value by bearing testament to a changeable past through 'these successive weldings of different styles'. 'Notre-Dame is not what could be called a complete, determinate, or classified monument,' the reader is told in one of several digressions that develop this key argument. 'Each face, each stone of this venerable monument is a page.'[28] If literature needed to trace the variability and specificity of history rather than standardize it, then the architecture of the past had to be preserved as part of this move to better understand society. This was an essential duty to fulfil if the populace was to be lifted out of ignorance and superstition. Ink and stone formed part of the same acts of self-expression and self-awareness. The cathedral is a unifying force. The reader is invited to climb the towers at Easter and behold the tumult of the city's bells ringing out, 'singing as one' in 'this city which has turned into an orchestra'.[29] From Notre-Dame's central vantage point, the disparate and the discordant were all connected.

For these reasons, Hugo had declared 'War on the Demolition Men!' in an 1825 argument that he would add to a later edition of the novel. Influenced by Nodier and himself uneasy at the devastation of the Napoleonic Wars, he deplored the 'vandalism' that had been inflicted upon buildings like Notre-Dame by the atheistic 'Cult of Reason' after 1789 and similar acts of cultural and economic short-termism. The cathedral had been stripped of its coloured stained-glass windows and central spire, among other 'mutilations', which Hugo's prose restored thanks to his research on medieval history. In the third volume of his enormous *History of France* later that decade, Jules Michelet wrote that he would have discussed Notre-Dame 'but someone has left such a mark on this monument, like a lion claiming its prize, that now no one dares touch it'.[30] So inviting was Hugo's 'cathedral of poetry', to use Michelet's wording, that it galvanized French public support for the preservation of historical monuments, paving the way for Eugène Viollet-le-Duc's major renovation of the cathedral (1844–64). Through his writing, Hugo helped to rebuild one of the world's most famous landmarks as we know it today.

More immediately, *Notre-Dame de Paris* provided Hugo with a repository for his marital concerns. Quasimodo's loneliness and Frollo's frustrated libido were obvious personal resonances for the snubbed husband who wrote to his wife that 'without you, this bed that you could be in (even though you no longer want to be, wicked woman!), this bedroom . . . it is all sad and mournful to me'.[31] Esmeralda's adolescent longing for the superficial Phoebus might also have implied some doubt over how much effort Hugo had been investing in his pursuit of fame, given that the captain's surname, Châteaupers, echoed that of his literary hero. But he had covered too much ground to retreat now.

With censorship eased under the July Monarchy, *A Duel Under Richelieu* was performed under the new title of *Marion de Lorme*. Hugo had chosen to work with the Théâtre de la Porte-Saint-Martin, which was more popular in its tastes than the Comédie-Française, but his use of verse did not fully connect with an audience more used to prose. The play's preface brimmed with optimism about the future, nevertheless, now that the July Revolution would give artists and audiences free rein, and that 'the wretched words for quarrelling – *classic* and *romantic*' would no longer be needed.[32] He called for a worthy French successor to Shakespeare, who would be to the Bard what Napoleon was to Charlemagne, exercising genius and bringing new glory to his country.

Hugo was being more brazen about the public role he saw for himself, but *Autumn Leaves* at the end of the year offered another well-received reminder that this occupation was first and foremost an artistic one. More emphatically than in *Orientalia*, he discussed how societies could rise and fall, but how poetry should never abandon its efforts to understand the human heart as a barometer for the world's perennial nature. *Autumn Leaves* turned away from society's material changes and looked inwards. It was to be a book whose pages fell like leaves from a tree and registered the poet's emotional cycles like the turning of the seasons. It was completed during the first of several annual family vacations to the Bertin family home. Nestled in an idyllic hamlet southwest of Paris, Les Roches became a new Feuillantines for Hugo, where nature's restorative powers could work upon him and soothe his worried mind: 'Here the soul contemplates, listens, adores, aspires,/ And pities the world, that strait and inane empire.'[33]

Nature's palliative effects refreshed Hugo's poetic vision as a viewpoint from which he could take in both the palpable and the intangible. The fifth and 29th poems in particular articulated how his line of sight shuttled between surface and depth in his communion with nature's unending transformations. 'What is Heard on the Mountain' depicts a poet listening atop a peak to two choruses: nature's call from the oceans, which sings the wonder of eternal creation, and man's murmurings from land, which express melancholy and irritation with this transience. The last stanza presents a mind taking greater flight than ever before to ponder the ultimate question: 'Why we are here,/ What in the end might be the point of all of this.' No clear answer is provided, but what has emerged by the poem's end is an intuitive understanding of joy and misery as interactive utterances from the same voice.

In 'Reverie's Slope', he therefore defended the poet's right to let himself slip into his thoughts and become absorbed by them in order to access this deeper knowledge. Sliding from the real world to an invisible realm, his mind ebbs like a river into a whirling mass of people and places, both present and past, which defies the clarity of visual representation: 'Soon all around me the dark shadows did accrue/ The horizon retreated, forms vanished from view.' Any reproduction of the experience must draw on the imagination's faculties and register 'the ineffable beside the invisible'. To render the feel of the shores at 'this dual sea of time and space', feeling is as integral as observation. The aftermath is as emotionally diverse as the expedition itself: 'Astounded, out of breath, knocked senseless, and terrified.' The line's mixed mood evinces that of the book's autumnal title, divulging a fear on Hugo's part that the lustre of his twenties was on the wane.

1832–5: Heading into Twilight

The volcano of social agitation that Hugo had sensed after the July Revolution erupted again in June 1832. Discontent with the regime's *juste milieu* had grown due to rising costs, a workers' revolt in Lyon and an outbreak of cholera in Paris. Hugo was working in the Tuileries Gardens the day that the republican uprising started. Drawn by the lure of history in the making, he had taken a closer look at the fighting that had broken out around nearby Les Halles but took cover when he got too close to one of the barricades.

The drama was over by the following evening. Louis-Philippe was better prepared for insurrection than his cousin had been, but 'all this blood-drenched lunacy'[34] reminded Hugo of the hostilities that the July Monarchy had failed to resolve and would later form one of the main episodes in *Les Misérables*.

At the end of the year, he had a confrontation of his own with the king's government when his play *The King Takes his Amusement* was censored. This verse drama was written at the same time over the summer as a prose play, *Lucrezia Borgia*. After the disputes surrounding *Hernani* and the lukewarm reception of *Marion de Lorme*, Hugo eyed up simultaneous success at the Comédie-Française and the Porte-Saint-Martin. He wanted the former to accept the modernization of tragedy and the latter to elevate popular melodrama. *The King Takes his Amusement* follows the efforts of an unsightly court jester, Triboulet, who seeks vengeance on King François I for the rape of his daughter, Blanche. Rushed preparation and set malfunctions did not make for a stellar opening night. François' vanity and especially Triboulet's insult of the king's courtly enablers as being the sons of unfaithful mothers guaranteed the play's demise, since gossip had long called into question the fidelity of Louis-Philippe's own mother. Hugo knew from his previous run-in with the censors that it would be in his interest to take the moral high ground. Just days before his court appeal, he published a preface defending his right to freedom of expression and his disappointment at seeing the July Monarchy take a step backwards. His efforts were in vain, but this time he renounced the entirety of his annual royal pension. The message was clear: Victor Hugo's integrity would not be compromised.

Lucrezia Borgia, on the other hand, which premiered in February 1833, avenged him with the biggest theatrical success of his lifetime. This play approached the themes of parental devotion, abuses of power and defective moral bearings from a different angle. Where Triboulet was a physically ugly father who was prepared to kill for his daughter's lost honour, Lucrezia was a beautiful but immoral mother who used her family's skills with poison to avenge herself for insults against her own dishonourable character. In the end, both parents are inadvertently responsible for the deaths of their children, but in Lucrezia's case the denouement was all the more sensational in its audience's eyes. Her son Gennaro refuses the antidote to the poison that will kill him along with his friends, and he runs Lucrezia through with his blade. With her last breath, she reveals that she is his mother. In addition to the talents of Mademoiselle George and Frédérick Lemaître in the main roles, the play benefitted from the Porte-Saint-Martin's resident composer, Alexandre Piccini, who wrote musical motifs for the characters that drew the audience further still into the action. Such was the effect that Hugo would stage another prose drama at the theatre, *Marie Tudor*, towards the end of the year. Taking Queen Mary i's repressive character, Hugo further explored the uncontrollable nature of human passions and the mismatch between moral idealism and social reality.

The betrayal, violence and grief at work in these plays reflected more than universal human malaise or national unrest. Hugo was coming to accept that his marriage to Adèle could never be the same and that his friendship with Sainte-Beuve was irrevocably broken. When he wrote to Sainte-Beuve that 'my consolation in this life is to have never been the first to desert a heart that loved me',[35] he could easily have been addressing Adèle. The family had recently moved to the Place Royale (today known as the Place des Vosges, the oldest planned square in Paris), but there would be no fresh start for the Hugos. Adèle's affair with Sainte-Beuve would cool over time and her marriage become amicable, but never again amorous. Love morphed into sentimentality. They managed to avoid the antipathy and implosion of his parents' relationship but not its disillusionment. Whether Hugo had been finding comfort elsewhere since the spring of 1830 is uncertain. There is no doubt, however, that in 1833 he began an extramarital affair of his own, which would last to the grave.

Juliette Drouet was a glamorous, dark-eyed actress who had been cast as Princess Negroni in *Lucrezia Borgia*. The nearly 27-year-old's acting skills were mediocre due to stage fright, but her presence was dazzling: 'a diamond that needs but a single ray of light to sparkle in a thousand ways', Hugo would later write.[36] He very quickly became enamoured, if nervous. Juliette took the initiative and instigated their first (sleepless) night together by writing the first of half a century's worth of daily correspondence. She shared his literary passions and emotional idealism, and even teased him that he initially could not keep pace with her own desires. It was a revelation for Hugo: 'When I am sad, I think of you, as we think of the sun in winter, and when I am happy, I think of you, as we think of shade in full sunlight.'[37] The woman he came to call 'Juju' brought him the purpose and reassurance that he longed for in a partner. Her lavish past as a courtesan also spurred his insecurity and jealousy, as well as his frustrations with her mounting debts. Juliette's Breton blood may have reminded Hugo of his mother, but it fired some heated arguments about her expensive lifestyle. When she ended one letter with the plea 'Whatever happens, let's love one another,'[38] she was indirectly recognizing that theirs would not always be a heavenly affair but that her commitment would be unwavering.

The clashes of the previous several years, combined with the reorganization of his personal life, encouraged Hugo to review his progress and signpost his current directions. The following year he published *Literature and Philosophy Mixed Together*, in which he assembled various critical essays written since 1819 to present the development of his ideas as a coherent process. In the case of his 1823 article on Scott, and with *Notre-Dame de Paris* obviously in mind, he added more precise comments about how contemporary writers could improve upon Scott's example. He felt that the lyric qualities of fiction could be heightened using a more expressive style

Léon Noël, *Juliette Drouet*, 1832, lithograph.

than Scott that would be 'at once dramatic and grand, picturesque but poetic'.[39]

Hugo's self-portrait in *Literature and Philosophy Mixed Together* was of a writer who believed in the need for art to pick up where Napoleon had left off and to fulfil the Revolution's promises of a new world. The title conveyed his discomfort with being defined by only one half of a binary: he did not like literary movements that saw art as needing to remain entirely removed from social reality, nor schools of thought such as the utopian socialist Saint-Simonians who characterized art's purpose as primarily social in nature. Neither the credos of 'art for art's sake' nor art as a cog in the social machine would suffice.

Next to his articles on figures like Scott and issues like national heritage appeared two recent essays that emphasized the role he saw for himself as a writer. The first used the death of a penniless young poet called Ymbert Galloix to speak out against poverty. Sidestepping the cliché of the forlorn young poet afflicted with Musset's melancholic *mal du siècle*, Hugo promoted a more socially contextualized response to the problem. The second essay discussed the liberal model of opposition that the comte de Mirabeau had bequeathed to history as one of the French Revolution's orators. Where Voltaire's philosophy was corrosive, Mirabeau's speeches were pulverizing, and both used their intellects to the same ends: 'Destroy the old orders and prepare the new ones.'[40] Both essays affirmed that the 'great man' of the nineteenth century needed to possess both conscience and eloquence. Mixing literary imagination with philosophical judgement, he had to avoid the singularities of abstract thought and prosaic politics.

Hugo's short story *Claude Gueux* (1834) and his prose drama *Angelo, Tyrant of Padua* (1835) maintained this artistically minded and morally inclined approach. The former returned to the subject of the penal system by taking liberties with the real-life story of a Parisian worker-turned-criminal. It underlined an increasingly prominent facet of Hugo's social thinking: society's collective responsibility to cure the disease of immorality, which could not simply be cut out like a tumour. 'The people are hungry and cold. Poverty pushes them to crime or vice . . . The laws you make, when you make them, are but palliatives or expedients.'[41] Another of his social concerns framed *Angelo* with the inequality between men and women. The jealous tyrant Angelo is married to the unhappy Catarina and has the courtesan Thisbe as his mistress. The low-born Thisbe's real love is reserved for the chaste Rodolfo, but he is secretly in love with Catarina. Thisbe sacrifices herself so that Rodolfo and Catarina can flee Angelo's wrath. Not only has she overcome her social antagonism towards the *podesta*'s wife by recognizing their shared plight in a male-dominated court, but she has chosen love over vengeance. In both *Claude Gueux* and *Angelo*, Hugo critiqued his society's moral assumptions about its outcasts and underclass. In the latter, he was also toying with his own divergent feelings as a rejected husband who was himself now unfaithful.

With these public and private concerns alive in his mind in 1835, the poems of *Twilight Songs* returned to the transitory qualities of his previous collection's autumnal character. Twilight, as the crepuscular moment of half-light and semi-darkness at dawn and dusk, was a pertinent image for France's equivocal position between absolutism and democracy, and for his own ambivalent emotions: what his preface pointed to as 'this mist in the world outside and this uncertainty within'. At a time of entrenched thinking that demanded definitive lines to follow, Hugo wanted to couple rather than divorce different elements, as dramatized in the first of forty poems, 'Prelude'. Unsure of whether the sun is rising or setting, its crossed rhymes suggest constant oscillation. Criticisms of greed and scarcity abounded in early verses such as 'On the Hôtel de Ville Ball', in which self-interested partygoers remain oblivious to the suffering around them, and 'Oh! Never Insult a Fallen Woman' ('Who knows under what burden the poor soul succumbs!').

The lyric themes of *Autumn Leaves* regarding nature, love and the passing of time also recurred, with the usual potency of his lexicon and metaphors, such as the descriptions of his verse as errant hailstones rapping against walls or of humanity's forehead teeming within the 'hideous vipers' of superstition.[42] Later poems such as 'Since My Lips Touched Your Still Full Cup', with its pulsating anaphora and exclamatory celebration of love, made no secret of his passion for Juliette, nor did a trio of verses hide his admiration of Adèle's nobility as a companion and mother. The contrasts of his outward and inward gazes as a poet, and of his appetites for excitement and tranquillity as a man, all remained connected but very much unsettled and in motion.

3

'I will set my frail barque onto the wrathful waves' (1836–51)

Hugo's description of himself as a fragile ship setting sail on an incensed sea comes from his poem to Eugène in the summer of 1837. His brother had died earlier that year at the Charenton asylum. 'To Eugène, Viscount Hugo' offers a cross section of Hugo's mind at a time when his forward momentum found itself compromised.[1] By the late 1830s, Hugo had conquered both poetry and the stage, as well as the less classical terrain of prose fiction, but his purpose now faltered. In fairness, any steps after achievements like the triumvirate of *Orientalia*, *Hernani* and *Notre-Dame de Paris* were bound to seem halting. Likewise, the early magic of a first love and fatherhood could not be conjured the same way again. The autumnal turn and dimmed light that had couched his recent poetry were reflective of his presentiment that the bright days of his youth were ending.

In a poem of over thirty sestains, his brother's death triggered emotions that were not without precedent in his writing: dejection at fate's cruelty, in this case Eugène's acute illness ('Since God, locking you away in the body's cage, / Gave to you, poor eaglet, wings but no eyes to gaze, / A soul without reason'); wistful affection for days gone by ('So much enduring charm! . . . Us two in the same bed, slumbering side by side'); and a need not to be forsaken ('Gentle and blonde companion of my childhood entire . . . You must still remember those verdant Feuillantines!'). The poet vows to carry on, but this commitment is curtailed by the contrast between boyhood fantasies of greatness and the toll they take: pointed attacks from rivals, and betrayals from friends, no doubt referencing how Sainte-Beuve had jealously turned on Hugo in his articles. The poet sees his brother at peace, whereas he is still caught up in the unstable currents of the here and now:

> And I will stay behind to suffer, work, and live;
> . . . But what labour it is! What tides and flow! Such spume!
> . . . Why make oneself worn out with passions so diverse?
> Why make for oneself a destiny so perverse?

When Hugo asks, 'Why does God put the best days of our life/ All at the very start?', it is clear that the backward glance which had served him well in tracking his progress was now prone to a downcast rather than upbeat nostalgia. He had not emerged from his battles unscathed.

Creeping feelings of fatigue and disillusionment were hard to avoid under a new regime that, by this time, had seen a succession of governments, four different uprisings and an attempted assassination of the king. While Hugo's marriage had ended up fragmenting rather than unifying his needs for belonging and passion, his country teetered along the July Monarchy's *juste milieu*, ever further from Napoleon's glory days but little closer to the democratic ideals of 1789. In a letter to the Martinican writer Louis de Maynard de Queilhe, a disenchanted Hugo observed that: 'Politics have not become more venerable since you left. Little men labouring over a small thing.'[2] The current climate did not lend itself to grandeur.

For the next fifteen years, Hugo's literary energies waned, his affections became more complicated and his family life was again struck by tragedy. Yet as this eventide drew in, there were new opportunities for recognition and self-expression. The period that saw Hugo's literary productivity noticeably decline, and which witnessed one of his personal life's most painful episodes, is the same stage of his career in which he joined various national institutions and his political influence broadened. The wealthier he became thanks to his earnings and financial investments, and the more closely he became involved with the French political class, the more convinced he was of the need for socio-economic and legislative reform. If these years heightened his anxiety over not fully identifying with who he had become, they also deepened his resolve to give such trepidation a more positive meaning in his vision of a free world.

1836–42: One of the 'Immortals'

Hugo's first two attempts to get elected to the Académie française in 1836 were unsuccessful, despite having the backing of names like Chateaubriand and Lamartine. Moreover, he had Juliette's devotion in his efforts to gather the necessary votes from existing Academicians. Adèle resented Juliette for the time and money that Hugo spent on her, as well as her reputation as a courtesan, which in her eyes tarnished her respected husband. Nonetheless, she made it clear that, in affairs of the heart, he was free to do as he pleased. 'As long as you are happy, so will I be . . . Never would I abuse the rights that marriage gives me over you. I like to think that you might be as free as a boy.'[3] It was therefore Juliette who rode in the carriage with Hugo, waited while he wooed potential supporters and then strategized with him on the way to the next meeting.

The lovers had tried to put their initial arguments behind them by going on vacation together two years beforehand to the Belgian border. It had been Hugo's first trip away from the Île-de-France region in almost a decade. Soon afterwards, however, they had engaged in a heated exchange over her costly debts. Juliette left him and Paris. A church-set reunion and a three-week Breton vacation brought concessions from both sides by allowing further dialogue. During his annual family holiday with the Bertins afterwards, Hugo installed Juliette and her nearly eight-year-old daughter Claire in a small house around 4 kilomteres (2.5 mi.) away from Les Roches. He met her halfway nearly every day in the woods, where they used a hollow chestnut tree as a postbox.

In the following two years, Juliette had renounced her old lifestyle to play a real-life Romantic heroine under Hugo's direction: the fallen woman redeemed through love and maternal duty. She now led an austere and sequestered existence in apartments he paid for that were close enough to his Paris home to allow him to divide his time. The man who would be perceived as one of nineteenth-century France's most prominent feminist allies was regrettably too suspicious of his lover's past to allow her to open her own post or leave the apartment without him, although he included a maid called Suzanne and some pets in the allowance. She had consoled herself in 'this tyranny that you exert over me' with his gifts of literary dedications and their holidays, which in 1837 took them on their first foreign trip, when they spent over a month together in Belgium.[4] A permanently available audience of one, Juliette had become Hugo's proofreader, secretary and even seamstress. Their correspondence reveals a mutually dependent and sometimes masochistic affair, with Juliette writing of being muzzled with kisses and a pained Hugo desperately begging her to love him always.[5] Before the decade was done, they would negotiate a private agreement – a moral marriage, as they called it – in which she promised never to take to the stage again and he vowed to fulfil all husbandly commitments, which included paying Claire's boarding school fees and taking care of both of them.

With two wives, two families, a republican streak curbed by his sympathy for political moderation and a career that was defined by both a rally against tradition and a desire to enter into France's pre-eminent literary institution, Hugo was trying to sail two courses.

His next book of poetry, *Inner Voices* (1837), listened to his heart's chatter and echoed this plurality. Grieving for his brother and prone to contrary desires, he created an idealized alter ego named Olympio to dialogue more openly with himself in one of the book's best-known poems, 'To Olympio'. Olympio consoles the confounded poet by reminding him of the need to sync his heart's rhythms with 'The ocean that breathes in and out just like a chest,/ Swelling and softening',[6] and to see contrasts not in isolation but turning through one another on fate's wheel. Running to 75 quatrains, 'To Olympio' was a lengthy but necessary reassurance in a volume that reaffirmed poetry's powers for moral and emotional arbitration. The preface reiterated that poetry was to be like God, 'one and inexhaustible'. In a reworking of the 1792 proclamation that the French Republic was 'one and indivisible', Hugo favoured creation's unstoppable spirit over the unbreakable structures dreamed of by men. To invoke this spirit, the poet had to tune into the three connected voices audible at home, through nature and on the streets. Autobiography, philosophy and history comprised the same epic melody. *Inner Voices* did not give Hugo's readers much new to listen to, but it did amplify his thinking.

His return to the stage the following year registered a more emphatic step forward by highlighting his social egalitarianism more assertively than in his previous dramas. *Ruy Blas* exemplified the allure of Romantic theatre to both well-heeled and popular audiences. Set in seventeenth-century Madrid (another of Hugo's historical Spanish settings), an honourable valet called Ruy Blas becomes embroiled in his callous master Don Salluste's revenge against the benevolent queen, Doña Maria. Salluste disguises Blas as a nobleman, knowing he secretly loves Doña Maria and will gain her favour. She in turn makes Blas the prime minister, and the 'earthworm in love with a star' champions worthy reforms,[7] only for Salluste to spring his trap to discredit the queen. The five-act structure, alexandrine verse and hero's eventual suicide gave the play its tragic credentials, while comic touches (including moments of buffoonery) and the plot's melodramatic features (such as stolen identities and betrayals) rounded out the breadth of appeal. By bringing the court's lowest and highest levels together through the central love story, Hugo offered a utopian vision of political power and the people's needs coming together.

Working with Dumas, he had used their cordial relations with the popular heir to the throne, the Duc d'Orléans, and his wife, an unashamed Hugo fan, to gain the Ministry of the Interior's permission to create a new theatre. It would artistically situate itself between the Comédie-Française and the Porte-Saint-Martin. *Ruy Blas* inaugurated the new Théâtre de la Renaissance and enjoyed a healthy run into 1839, but critics disliked the plot's implausibility and complained that Hugo was recycling Romantic platitudes rather than inventing fresh material. Without Sainte-Beuve to draw fire in the press, Hugo was more vulnerable to such attacks. Furthermore, he was losing some of his fan base: the ethos of 'art for art's sake' had been attracting numerous younger writers since Gautier's famous preface to *Mademoiselle de Maupin* (1835), which itself built on ideas from *Orientalia* and *Autumn Leaves*.

Hugo's notes for his plays revealed more frequent alterations and indecision since he had written *Marie Tudor*, and the writing of a new play, *The Twins*, proved more difficult than hoped.[8] The personally sensitive subject-matter of the legend of the man in the iron mask, in which one brother is feted at the expense of the other's misfortune, had made the process yet more challenging, and Hugo dropped the project in the summer of 1839. Shortly afterwards, he took his annual vacation with Juliette on a nearly two-month trip through Switzerland and the Midi de France along the Rhône. His membership of the Ministry of Public Instruction's committee for the preservation of national history gave his imagination a more research-orientated bent on such trips and the chance to refocus. Doting letters to his family, in which he shared his sights through descriptions and drawings, show that his affections continued to run parallel rather than sequentially while vacationing. 'My Didine' (Léopoldine), 'my Charlot' ('little' Charles), 'my Toto' (Victor) and 'my Dédé' (Adèle junior) were always on his mind, as was 'my Adèle'.

The following year, after two more failed campaigns to get into the Académie française, Hugo presented *Sunlight and Shadows* as the final installation of the series begun with *Autumn Leaves* and continued by *Twilight Songs* and *Inner Voices*. This volume would be the weightiest of the four. He reinvested in both the significance and the potential of his poetic imagination as a 'civilizing' force that would add to the 'Poem of Mankind' developed by Virgil, Dante, Milton and Byron. Comments in the preface that his 'horizon has expanded, the sky become more azure' confirmed that he would persevere in augmenting his mind's reach and scrutiny, come what may, and continue to yoke together humanity, nature and society in order to understand the span of God's Creation. The first five stanzas of the opening poem, felicitously titled 'The Poet's Function', delineated two possible trajectories for the poet: into the crowd and

Victor Hugo, 'Lucerne. What I can see from my window', 13 September 1839, ink. Hugo frequently sketched on his travels, and he included this one for his daughter Léopoldine in a letter to his wife.

towards social interests, or away 'from our tempests' and into nature's reposeful embrace. The poet responds in the subsequent 34 verses that nature remains an essential balm, but that 'in this intrepid century' his gifts are needed to illuminate a better world. With 'his footing here, his gaze elsewhere', he had to situate the mortal world within a broader sphere.

The volume's most reproduced poem utilized this visionary ability and articulated the poignancy of his feelings about how swiftly the past could dwindle. He again called upon Olympio as a way of looking beyond himself. What he saw was a heart that was no longer in the initial throes of love. Written in the contemplative alexandrine form, 'The Melancholy of Olympio' took Hugo's readers to the zenith of his lyricism by capturing the beats of nature's 'universal heart'. Where Lamartine's hugely popular 'The Lake' (1820) had offered an elegy for a love cut short by death, this longer poem meditated on how love cannot maintain its early intensity in a naturally transient world. The pale figure wanders through an unspoilt vale, where 'the shades of bygone days' cast themselves across his memory as he tries to root out remnants of a past relationship with an unnamed lover. Eroticism pervades some of his sensations (a breeze 'swaying the rose or stirring the tall beech'), but the sights have ultimately changed:

> Little of what we were remains alive.
> Here the forest has shrunk, there it has spread:
> Our gathered memories scatter in the wind
> Like a mere pile of ashes, cold and dead.
> . . . Has our time passed?
> Can nothing be brought back by our frail cries?[9]

Inspired by the Bièvre valley and privately dedicated to Juliette, the poem ends by recording how, even as the soul descends crestfallen into the night, the power of memory gives an afterlife to past feelings. Hugo would not let go of his past cares, but nor was he blind to his present confusions.

Early in 1841, he was finally elected as one of the Académie's 'immortals'. The popularity of *Sunlight and Shadows* had helped, as had a collection of his odes to Napoleon in honour of the return of the emperor's remains to Paris that winter, which had been another of the July Monarchy's attempts to weld France's historical differences into a coherent whole. Imperial nostalgia and nationalist sentiment had intensified during the previous year. The French government had backed Muhammad Ali Pasha's claim to Egypt, but the other European powers had supported the Ottoman Empire. To avert war, Louis-Philippe eventually accepted the settlement of the 'Eastern Question' by the same coalition of nations that had humiliated France at the Congress of Vienna. Against this backdrop, Hugo took his election ceremony to the Académie française as an opportunity to figuratively wave the French Tricolor before an excited audience, which included his family and Juliette. France had a proud history in leading civilization towards a more radiant future, he insisted, meaning that 'France is an integral part of Europe'.[10] Where Napoleon had tried to fulfil the Revolution's mission through military might, modern France needed its most commanding minds to do so through the empire of ideas. Such was the poet's function and his glory.

Hugo turned to his notes from his travels with Juliette to promote France's continental importance through a new medium: travel writing. Published in 1842, *The Rhine* presented itself as a collection of nearly forty letters written during a journey through the Rhineland that recalled the itineraries of other Romantics taking their Grand Tour. It became a popular guidebook, but Hugo's goals were not commercial. *The Rhine* was a bespoke display case for his current political vision rather than an accurate travelogue: he reordered the chronology of his three different holidays through the region since 1838 to suit the book's imagined route and fabricated

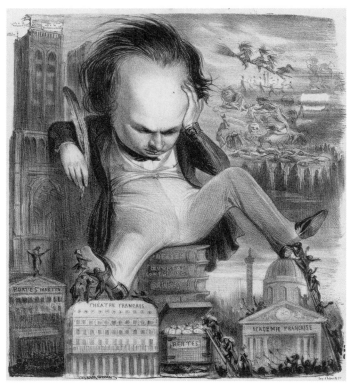

Benjamin Roubaud, *The Charivaric Pantheon*, 22 December 1841. Hugo leans back in contemplation against Notre-Dame de Paris cathedral while various characters of his swirl to the right. Beneath his feet lie the Porte Saint-Martin and Comédie-Française theatres (left) and the Académie française (right), as well as an overflowing chest of earnings. Crowning the image, the excessively large forehead symbolizes Romantic genius.

several entries, including a visit to Speyer. These letters to an unnamed friend, such as that describing the Rhine Falls, displayed many of the literary features seen in Hugo's fiction to convey how his imagination had thrived in these unfamiliar places: single-sentence paragraphs to control the dramatic pace and to draw his reader's eye amidst the more heaving streams of thought ('I went to the very edge of the balcony and leant out onto the rock'); verbless phrases to concentrate the mind on a particular sight rather than action ('Marvellous spectacle! Horrifying tumult!'); and the use of resemblance to suggest a more far-seeing narrative vision ('You think that you can see before you the four fulgurant wheels of the Lord's storm-chariot').[11]

Through Hugo's eyes, the Rhine's geography and history bore testament to a universal creativity that defined Europe's past and future as the continent's central artery. The letters were bookended by two essays that superimposed a united Europe with France at its heart. Above all, he envisaged the Rhine as an axis of power based on cultural as well as economic community between the French and the Germans, continuing the work of Charlemagne and Napoleon. This bond would more effectively combat social inequality and guarantee peace by keeping the power of both Britain and Russia in check. Lamartine wrote to him that 'The King will make you a peer and we will make you a minister' as a result of such arguments.[12] Heartened by these interventions, Hugo prepared another play to dramatize his political programme. Since the Théâtre de la Renaissance had unfortunately not survived due to financial failings, he returned to the Comédie-Française. The new year would, however, brutally cut short this rediscovered flow of force.

1843–7: Loss, Love and Lordship

Premiering in March, *Les Burgraves* has often been remembered as a spectacular flop, in part because after 1843 Hugo would never again stage a new dramatic work. That is not to say, as can be quickly assumed, that theatre ceased to be of interest to him. His later interventions against theatre censorship and his more experimental theatrical writings during exile put paid to that argument. Given the tragedy to come later in 1843, which would inevitably taint the play's memory, it would also be hasty to surmise that this play alone was the root cause of some theatrical adieu. Nevertheless, *Les Burgraves* registered his career's least sizeable box-office income, despite a run of 33 performances.

The public had begun to tire of Romantic dramas, for the moment at least, so Hugo attempted an epic verse melodrama. Set along the thirteenth-century Rhine, the plot fixed upon the feudal barons of the title and a family rivalry in which the noble centenarian Job has been usurped by a younger and more egotistical generation. The Heppenheff burg prays for release from their tyranny, which comes from the returning Holy Roman Emperor, Barbarossa, who was believed to be dead after Job's rebellion. Quite aside from the unbelievable character ages and convoluted familial intrigue, much of the drama pivoted on events from the past, which had to be recounted at length by the characters rather than acted out with more emotional immediacy on stage. By the time Barbarossa and Job reconcile, the audience had little interest, even if Hugo offered a more optimistic denouement than his usual sacrifice of young heroes in the name of love. It was a major disappointment, especially as the play's preface set out his idea of a united Europe, advocating European civilization in the way Aeschylus and Virgil had accepted Greece and Rome as their calling. Hugo's literary works had been traversing this continent and its history since his career began, covering Britain, France (and the Antilles), Germany,

Italy, Norway and Spain. The Rhine's image of a Franco-German confederation was evolving into a more inclusive entity whose main goal would be collective prosperity rather than just national security, but *Les Burgraves* was not an effective catalyst for this fraternal dream.

Being abandoned by his audience exacerbated the reverberations of other recent losses. The Duc d'Orléans, whose marriage to a German princess offered a symbol of Franco-German cooperation, had died in a carriage accident the previous summer. More upsettingly, Hugo's eighteen-year-old daughter Léopoldine had married a man named Charles Vacquerie three weeks before *Les Burgraves* debuted. She was to make her life in his family home near Le Havre, around 200 kilometres (125 mi.) northeast of Paris. A blessing following the loss of Hugo's first-born, Léopold, 'Didine' had been an object of particular affection for her father, especially after her mother's affair. Juliette held her poet's head to her chest the day after the wedding: 'My beloved child is leaving me,' he wept. He left Juliette in no doubt as to what he needed: 'Always love me this way! Charm me, caress me, support me, console me. Be my consolation as you are my beauty: fill all my heart's voids with love!'[13] Rheumatism in his hands and a flaring up of his sore eyes confirmed that a getaway was needed. In mid-July the couple headed south to the Basque Country, where Hugo rekindled his childhood memories of Spain, then visited the spa of Cauterets in the Hautes-Pyrénées before heading back along the Bay of Biscay. He sent the usual letters and sketches to his children, recounting how his Spanish was coming back to him, but making no mention of his dutiful travelling companion.

Taking an afternoon beer in Rochefort on 9 September, Hugo and Juliette sat down to read the papers. Dumbstruck, he pointed to his copy of *Le Siècle*. It had been announced that on 4 September Léopoldine, her husband, his uncle and a young cousin had all drowned in a yachting accident not far from Villequier on the way back to Le Havre. He would not be able to get back to Paris

Auguste de Châtillon, *Léopoldine Hugo Reading the Book of Hours*, c. 1835, oil on canvas.

until three days later. 'My God!' he wrote to Adèle, who had been staying in Le Havre. 'What have I done to you! My heart is broken . . . '[14] His ambiguous outburst implied a guilty instinct that the tragedy was some form of punishment, which only sharpened once he returned to his family. He had missed the burial on 6 September. Léopoldine had been found in the arms of her husband who had died trying to save her; she had been three months pregnant.

Anything associated with her instantly became a precious artefact to her grieving parents, including a lock of her hair, her bridal wreath and the dress she was wearing on the day of the accident. Her father could not bring himself to visit her grave for another three years.

By the end of 1843, he was finding solace with a married woman he had met at one of Paris's salons, the 23-year-old Léonie Biard, née d'Aunet. Her name and age suggested a potential substitute for Léopoldine, but his desires had a far less paternal character. Blonde and graceful, Léonie possessed an imaginative and assertive character, having been the only woman on a scientific expedition to Spitsbergen when she accompanied the expedition's painter, Auguste Biard. Her unhappy marriage to Biard gave her something in common with Juliette and so many of Hugo's heroines as a woman apparently in need of vindication through love. Hugo took to his new purpose with the passion of someone who had been longing for a new dawn. Four years earlier, he had made a note of the working hours of two different prostitutes. They would not be the last. It is impossible to know for sure why he recorded such information: to find sexual relief or to give alms (or both)? Whatever the truth, Hugo undeniably looked upon his own libido as an explosive force. According to Olympio's observations, the poet had not dared approach Juliette when he first saw her 'because a powder keg is afraid of the spark'.[15] A scene in his notes from the early 1830s intimates his self-awareness as much as his humour. A feckless man asks whether a soothsayer's advice to 'be careful of your appendage' would have been more appropriate for something with a tail like a fox or comet.[16] The urges that the experienced Juliette had reignited seemed to be burning beyond her control, and she complained that her cat spent more time in her bed than Hugo did.

A series of poems that Hugo wrote about Léonie during their first year together, and which were mostly published posthumously in *The Whole Lyre*, attested to his newfound exhilaration. These differed from works he had written for Adèle and Juliette, favouring swifter metres and shorter verses, and centring more readily on pleasurable sensation than on noble or melancholic feeling. The poet is no longer the child-god Cupid, 'feeble and naked', but 'a proud knight, his visor lowered', who 'fights', 'strikes' and 'triumphs' when he sees his lover without her clothes, as she often is in these verses, all for 'that sweet abandon, known only to the angels' as her face becomes flush with pink.[17] Léonie offered him escape from a deflated marriage, a mellowed extramarital relationship, an exacting career and the purgatory of grief. She also ensured that his use of sexual pleasure as a remedy for personal malaise and a spur for his sense of self would become more entrenched in his behaviour as his forties progressed. Sometimes before posting his love letters to her, Hugo copied out those he found to be the most affecting and added pre-emptive disclaimers such as 'he said to her' on his duplicate, as if recounting someone else's story. He was protecting himself from discovery but subtly fracturing his self-identity further.[18]

A public embarrassment in the summer of 1845 showed his inability to close off the different paths he was now walking. In April the king appointed him to the peerage in the Upper Chamber of Parliament. He was already a regular face at the king's bourgeois court but his new status gave him deeper entry into the power base of Louis-Philippe's reign. It also gave him invaluable protection when he and Léonie were caught in flagrante delicto on 4 July after her husband had hired a private detective. Biard pressed charges. Léonie was imprisoned for adultery for two months, after which she was forced to spend several months in a convent. Hugo's peerage exempted him from prosecution but made him an even greater target for ridicule in the press, yet not even this humiliation lessened his reluctance to break with either of his mistresses or with his wife. Towards the end of the previous year, he had spent several months with Juliette decorating her new apartment. He placated her suspicions that something was awry with fresh declarations of love and with his permission to go out unescorted. Since he still bought her newspapers, he managed to hide the story from her while begging forgiveness from his wife for this mortifying episode. Adèle, for her part, took pity on Léonie and visited her, believing her to be a worthier mistress than her husband's other 'angel'.

Encouraged by his fellow peers to lay low, Hugo's first interventions in the Chamber did not come until early 1846. He would not be an idle patrician. He addressed the question of intellectual property, then he implored the government to denounce the Austrian suppression of the Peasant Uprising against serfdom in partitioned Poland. This March speech contained two integral ideas in his politics: the defence of the democratic right to self-determination and the recognition that a great nation's power had to be moral rather than simply military. In June, he unsuccessfully pleaded for life imprisonment instead of the death sentence on behalf of one of the king's would-be assassins.

The farce of 1845 was giving way to a historical drama, but later that same month he found himself in a tragedy once again when Juliette's daughter Claire succumbed to tuberculosis. She was a similar age to Léopoldine when she died. Attending Claire's funeral granted him the kind of emotional release that he had been denied when he had missed Léopoldine's burial, and the following autumn he joined his wife and remaining daughter in Villequier for the first time on their annual pilgrimage to her grave. At the same time, the parental grief that had reinforced his marital bonds with Adèle now had a similar effect on his relationship with Juliette.

Neither the dignity of his new political station nor the sobriety of his mourning eased his restlessness, however. Cryptic references in his journal strongly suggest that he was continuing to enjoy the company of other women. One of these was the actress Alice Ozy in 1847, much to the chagrin of her admirer, Hugo's eldest son Charles. In an ever-materialistic France in which the power of the banks and the stock markets had been steadily rising, Hugo may also have been quietly paying into the sex trade. His possible motivations were multiple and are still speculated over: a need to suspend his feelings by becoming mindful only of his body; a compulsive desire to test his free will; and an attraction to unconditioned and involuntary behaviour.[19] His reputation for gallantry is such that the slightest ambiguous mention of a woman in his private records has often been taken to imply a sexual encounter, although the evidence is ultimately dependent on how such references are deciphered.[20] What is certain is his fascination with the female form: 'Oh God! Joy, ecstasy, stupor,/ The body's exquisite beauty!'[21] His suspected preferences for the visuality and tactility of the striptease in such encounters would have derived as much from this rapture as from any prudence in limiting intercourse in nineteenth-century Paris, which was not known for its high standards of sexual health.

Hugo's roster of new books during this period – a conspicuous zero between 1843 and 1852 – may look apt for a writer whose time had been swallowed up by political duty, personal commitments and fleeting dalliances. Nevertheless, his literary imagination, although slack, was neither dormant nor pedestrian. Albeit slowly, he was laying the groundwork for later success, including what in exile would become his two most popular works. He wrote far fewer verses (one biographer helpfully estimates an average of only one poem per fortnight from 1843 to 1848)[22] and was unsure of what to do with them, so he chose to hold them back as he had done with other pieces since the late 1830s. In particular, Claire's death prompted a spurt of mournful verse that would feed the supply to *Contemplations* in the mid-1850s.[23]

He had also begun writing fiction again. His new novel's central concerns of social and moral redemption revealed a writer who, for personal as well as patriotic reasons, was thinking about absolution for the past. Begun in November 1845 with the working title of *Jean Tréjean*, it was to be the story of 'a saint, a man, a woman, and a doll', as he had jotted across the back of an envelope. Each of these figures was inspired by real-life happenings. In the late 1820s, he had read the newspaper story of Pierre Maurin, a convict who had spent five years in the *bagne* at Toulon for stealing bread, and who became an honourable soldier after being shown kindness by a Bishop Miollis in Digne. Hugo's ongoing research into prison life, and his pity for another bread thief that he saw being taken into custody in 1846, provided further material, as did his contact with Eugène-François Vidocq, the delinquent criminal famously turned criminal investigator. The woman was to be another of Hugo's fallen heroines. Her plight was drawn from the police's treatment of a prostitute whom Hugo had seen assailed in the snow in 1841, and whose conduct he adamantly defended.[24] The doll (one of the nicknames he had given Léopoldine) referred to the woman's innocent daughter, and he asked both Juliette and Léonie to write out their experiences of convent life to help describe her upbringing.

By the end of 1847, he had a contract with Gosselin for what was now *Les Misères*, or *The Miseries*. By referencing Eugène Sue's wildly successful serial novel *The Mysteries of Paris* (1842–3) in the new title, he wanted to step back to the forefront of popular fiction which had recently been occupied by Sue and friends like Balzac and Dumas. But he stopped writing when the revolutionary events of 1848 became more urgent then those on the page.

1848–51: *Le peuple*

Les Misères reflected Hugo's belief that literature could bring about change in modern civilization. Socio-economic restructuring would only go so far if there was no programme for the reform of human character to ensure that such change would be deep and lasting. This kind of reform hinged on the differentiation between the populace, which inclined towards self-interest and anger, and the people, which was 'all those who lean towards the good and the just', as he pointed out to the editor of a working-class newspaper.[25] His aversion to the former could not diminish his love for the latter, he added. Moreover, these feelings did not code the divide between the rank and file of society and its elites. The distinction he cited was moral, not class-based. The question was not whether someone was worker or bourgeois, outcast or paragon: it was whether they, like the novel's hero Jean Tréjean, could exceed purely material needs and acknowledge the universal humanity enshrined in the Revolution's core principles. In 1848, Hugo's distrust of the populace set him against the barricades that rose up in Paris; only three years later, his affinity with the people placed him on the opposite side of those ramparts after a defiant and definitive move to the political centre-left.

By the start of 1848, France was beset by crisis. The 1840s railway boom had collapsed, wiping out savings and businesses, and a poor harvest in 1846 had sent wheat and bread prices soaring, constraining spending and contributing to a manufacturing slump. Rising working-class unemployment and increased middle-class anxiety did not bode well, especially when the parliamentary electoral system remained hugely unrepresentative and enfranchised less than 1 per cent of the population. When the government clamped down on the opposition's 'banquet campaign' of political gatherings, a revolution broke out in Paris and forced Louis-Philippe to abdicate. On 26 February – Hugo's 46th birthday – the Second Republic was declared. Lamartine organized a provisional government that would announce universal male suffrage, the assurance of jobs through national workshops and the abolition of both slavery and the death penalty for political offences.

Hugo heard one street-fighter proclaim, 'It's 1830!' 'No,' he wrote. 'In 1830, there was the Duc d'Orléans to follow Charles x. In 1848, after Louis-Philippe there is a gap.'[26] With no single figure to steady France's course forward, he feared the rise of radical socialism.

Because the peerage had been abolished, he ran for election to the Constituent Assembly. He gravitated towards the emerging 'Party of Order', the conservative and moderate coalition that had won votes by promising to keep the republicans and socialists in check. Once elected, he decried the national workshops as costing a fortune but generating no actual jobs or long-term growth. When the government closed them down, a working-class uprising erupted in Paris on 23 June. A stage of siege was declared and emergency powers were granted to the minister of war, Louis-Eugène Cavaignac. 'What an awful business!', Hugo wrote to Adèle during the fighting. 'It's sad to think that all this blood flowing on both sides is decent and noble.'[27] He accepted his parliamentary duty as one of five dozen representatives to re-establish order. Amidst the gunfire, he helped coordinate the military efforts to break the barricades in the Faubourg du Temple and Saint-Antoine. What he experienced did nothing to make the general's son question whether he should have followed his father into the army. 'I was able to be the man of force . . . I will never be the man of violence.'[28]

Hugo's conscience was clear, but his heart was heavy, as he would recall in *Les Misérables* when he weighed up the horror of street-fighting during the 1832 insurrection by referring to the June Days. 'It had to be fought, and that was a duty, because the riot was aimed at the Republic. But what was June 1848, when it all comes down to it? A revolt of the people against themselves.' His criticism of the way the victors disparaged the fallen stressed his overriding sense that guilt for this bloodshed could not be neatly apportioned. Micro-aggressions in the use of words like scum or plebs, which were favoured by the well-to-do to demonize the lower classes rather than recognize any validity to their grievances, 'register the fault of those in power more than the fault of those who suffer'.[29] The government's extensive reprisals – around 25,000 arrests, almost half of which resulted in prison sentences, deportations or executions – treated the symptoms of France's social problems rather than their causes. Worse, General Cavaignac continued to preside over the Executive Committee and curtailed press freedoms to avoid further disorder.

Hugo had little time to lament Chateaubriand's death on 4 July. He lobbied for Paris's theatres to be reopened, then defended freedom of speech, knowing that Cavaignac, as the man associated with the ruthless repression of the June Days, could never heal France's wounds. Rather than support Lamartine, who had been out of his depth, Hugo warmed to Napoleon's nephew, who had returned to France after two failed coups the previous decade. Louis-Napoleon Bonaparte's family name, defence of the working class and attacks on social privilege made him the ideal foil to Cavaignac. Hugo announced his support that autumn in *L'Événement* (The Event), the daily newspaper that had been launched in the summer by his two sons and by two of his biggest admirers, the writers Paul Meurice and Auguste Vacquerie (Léopoldine's brother-in-law). The paper's epigraph was eminently Hugolian: 'Vehement hatred of anarchy; tender and profound love of the people.' Louis-Napoleon won the December elections by a landslide.

Hugo was elected to the new Legislative Assembly in May 1849 as one of hundreds of representatives for the Party of Order, but fretted over the erosion of the political centre-ground in an assembly that was dominated by conservative forces. In July, he attacked the paltry effort that had been made to abolish poverty and supported Armand de Melun's housing proposals. The Rights of Man gave all individuals their dignity, which was contradicted for many by the reality of their material misery. Hugo bombarded the government with examples of its failings, such as entire families living in cramped abodes and wearing rotting rags, or a mother and her four children rooting through the rubbish dump and offal houses at Montfaucon for food. 'You have done nothing while the people suffer! You have done nothing while below you there is a part of the country in despair!'[30]

The next month, he used his opening speech as the elected president of the Paris Peace Congress to reaffirm this message of unity, surpassing not only class borders but national ones as well. Coining the phrase 'the United States of Europe', he envisaged a significant step forward in the fight against inequality: a continent of free trade and movement, bound by a common currency and a shared sense of history, with military budgets and tax revenues redirected towards education and technology. Both speeches were typical of Hugo's oration: rhetorically frank and meticulously prepared through research and redrafting. They mimicked Mirabeau's calm but forceful tone, although they were also lyrical and rehearsed to the point where they could feel overly austere, if not anxious.[31]

The dramatist was not, by all accounts, a natural actor on stage, but it was the reviews that mattered. By the following summer, Hugo was hailed by the Left, which had steadily increased its share of the vote but lost its leader, Alexandre-Auguste Ledru-Rollin, who had been forced into exile. Hugo had been especially dismayed by Louis-Napoleon's tacit support for Pope Pius ix against Italian republicans during the ongoing French siege of Rome, and later by the Falloux Law, which was to place the responsibility for national education back in the clergy's hands. His speech in January 1850 against the Law sensationally accused the Right of being a parasitic disease afflicting the Christian faith: 'You are not believers, but sectarians of a religion you do not understand.'[32] Not only had his time in the Assembly hardened his commitment to key republican tenets such as social welfare, secular education, national suffrage and freedom of speech, but it had tightened the connections in his thinking between the French Republic and the Gospels as symbols of a universally democratic humankind. Hugo's break with the Right looked irreversible when new laws disenfranchised over a third of the electorate and censored the press and the theatres. These laws effectively denied the freedom to vote and to write openly.

Louis-Napoleon's own frustrations towards factions within the Party of Order and on the Left posed another challenge. He knew that the 1848 constitution restricted his presidential powers and that the 1850 electoral changes risked depriving him of popular legitimacy. The self-titled 'Prince-President' had been slowly bolstering his national appeal and bringing the armed forces on side as a natural-born leader whose energies were dedicated to the country's needs rather than to the Assembly's political allegiances. His desire for a constitutional amendment to enable a second term in office alarmed Hugo. In his impassioned speech of 17 July 1851, which lasted for nearly four hours due to recurrent interruptions, Hugo attacked those who would poison France with the moral cholera of anti-republicanism. He centred his ire directly on the chief of state: 'Because we had Napoleon le Grand, must we now have Napoleon le Petit?!'[33] The uproar in the Assembly lasted for several minutes; the moniker would stick to Louis-Napoleon for much longer. The demeaning comparisons with the original Napoleon were as much a reminder of Hugo's own convictions as a flaying of the president. Imitation and a return to the past would not mark out a man of the nineteenth century for greatness.

Hugo's elected status protected him from any direct return fire, but *L'Événement* had no such indemnity. The previous month, Charles Hugo had been handed a six-month prison sentence for condemning capital punishment and was remanded in custody at the end of July. One by one over the next two months, Hugo's youngest son (who now went by the forename François-Victor to avoid confusion with his father), Meurice and Vacquerie were sent to join Charles in the Conciergerie in central Paris for disrespecting the government. The conditions were not harsh: Hugo and other guests, including female company, dined with them regularly. Nevertheless, his family was being symbolically punished for following him into battle.

Hugo was also tackling a more domestic predicament, to which his July speech might have owed some of its exacerbated tone. In June, another of his inner circle who had seen a prison cell because of him, Léonie, had posted Juliette evidence of her affair with Hugo, hoping to force his hand. His first mistress had often suspected infidelity, but she was crushed to have proof of a younger rival and of how Léonie had been befriended by Adèle when she herself had always kept a respectful distance. A stoic but fateful Juliette rejected Hugo's immediate offer to break with Léonie and instead proposed a grace period of several months in which he would have to choose between them. It was a more effective tactic than Léonie's, as Juliette refused to exert any right over him at a time when he was increasingly being compelled to take political action.

Both quandaries came to a head in December, when Louis-Napoleon undertook his *coup d'état* on the anniversary of both his uncle's imperial coronation and the stunning victory at Austerlitz. The president had failed to win a large enough majority to amend the constitution and, in October, the Assembly's rejection of his move to restore universal suffrage strengthened his popular support. On 2 December, troops occupied strategic positions in Paris, arrested opposition leaders and proclaimed a series of edicts to establish Louis-Napoleon's rule, including the dissolution of the Assembly and the restoration of universal male suffrage. Hugo quickly formed a resistance committee with other like-minded parliamentarians and issued appeals for Paris to take up arms. Learning that his home was under surveillance, he went to Juliette. His instinct to go to the woman who had devotedly watched his speeches in the Assembly, copied out his writing and been part of his life for nearly two decades suggests that the constancy of their relationship had won out over the passions of his affair with Léonie. Certainly, it would be Juliette's efforts in remaining at his side and helping to arrange various boltholes that he would acknowledge in his later accounts, with no mention of Léonie.

The coup was too well orchestrated – and Parisians too disillusioned after the June Days – for the resistance to succeed, but it did give Hugo's conscience an air of moral invincibility. 'We do not even have the pleasure of being oppressed by something great.'[34] On 3 December, he was shocked by the death of another representative, Jean-Baptiste Baudin, who was shot on a barricade in the Faubourg Saint-Antoine (a location that Hugo had argued for among the other resisters); the following afternoon, he was horrified by the carnage at a barricade near the Boulevards, where he was shown the body of a seven-year-old boy who had been shot twice in the head. For Hugo, Louis-Napoleon's regime was not only illegal, it was now murderous. He went into hiding until Juliette obtained a friend's passport to enable him to escape to Brussels disguised as a worker on 11 December. She followed a few days later. The writer who had been part of France's literary and political establishment over the past decade was now its most famous exile, but Hugo was confident that his frail barque had history in his favour. 'We are in an era of light and a century of darkness, depending on which side of us faces the truth.'[35]

4

'I feel like I am atop life's true summit' (1852–70)

With the distance of exile came fresh perspective for Hugo, resulting in this feeling he described in 1854 of attaining a more revealing vantage point than ever before. History granted him his turn in exile just as it had Chateaubriand and Napoleon, not to mention Ovid and Dante. Heading away from the streets and into the desert he had imagined in 'The Poet's Function', he was freed from the cut and thrust of life in Paris. His poetic mind found stimulation in the physical and psychological geography of exile: in the landscapes and seascapes of the Channel Islands, and in the experience of solitude and withdrawal on foreign soil so close to his home country.

Both materially and mentally, exile was an unprecedentedly liminal experience for Hugo. It was akin to the half-light of daybreak and other such perpetually transitional phases that had a freeing effect on his imagination. His visionary faculties benefitted hugely from this contingency at a stage of his life when he was faced with his own mortality. His parents had been 49 and 54 when they died; Eugène had been 36; and Abel would pass at 56 in February 1855. As he stepped into his fifties watching the Second Empire ascend, the last Hugo brother feared that his time was passing.

Surrounded by the surging ocean and caught in the flux of history's drama, Hugo found himself at the unstable boundary between life and death, torn between feelings of belonging and estrangement. The view was compelling. 'I can see the true lineaments of everything that men call facts, history, happenings, success, catastrophes – the enormous machinery of Providence.'[1] Anticipating that his detractors would dismiss him as having his head in the clouds, he pre-emptively responded that clouds were also where thunder was made.[2] In turn, his writing pushed further along the 'slope of reverie' from *Autumn Leaves* and towards the vistas that were made accessible through nature's infinite power.

This far-seeing outlook was supported by the renewed sense of purpose that exile gave him as the truth-giving poet who chooses what is right over what is convenient. Writing from Brussels, he reported that 'never have I felt my heart to be lighter or more content'.[3] Upbeat declarations like this were not meant as bandages for his wounds in the immediate aftermath of Louis-Napoleon's coup, but as proof of robust health. 'Our two sons in prison and me in exile: the situation is unkind, but good. A little frost strengthens the harvest.'[4] Hugo found equanimity in the belief that 'it is not me who has been outlawed, it is liberty . . . I fought, I did my duty; I am defeated but happy.'[5] The climate on the moral high ground was as bracing as it was harsh.

What had happened in France was 'the perfection of infamy' in his view. Louis-Napoleon had won over 90 per cent of the popular vote in a constitutional referendum that was held barely three weeks after the coup, but 'were there to have been yet more zeroes after this figure of 7,500,000 votes, I would not trust such a lot of nothings'.[6] Hugo had his doubts about the referendum's nature and its outcome, but his point was to weigh the scales of justice rather than ascertain electoral statistics. No sum or mass could counter the weight of a clear conscience. Similarly, no military could combat a poet with ink in his bottle.

The duration and accomplishments of Hugo's exile make it his life's most mythic episode. It feeds into the same French patriotism as the Resistance efforts during the Nazi Occupation.

His uncompromising opposition to Louis-Napoleon and his excoriating attacks on the new regime were republicanism in action, determinedly pushing back against the weight of the times in the name of the Revolution's ideals:

> Only a thousand left? I'm with them, then!
> Were there a hundred, still I'd brave the Hun;
> I'd be the tenth, if there were only ten;
> If there were only one, I'd be that one![7]

In exile, he solidified his reputation worldwide as an indefatigable voice for tolerance, social welfare and solidarity.

His moral force was inseparable from his buoyant creativity throughout this period, which manifested itself both on the page and off it, and which brought his two most commercially successful books to fruition in the poems of *Contemplations* and in the chapters of his magnum opus *Les Misérables*. His refusal of Louis-Napoleon's offer of amnesty to exiles in 1859 importantly preserved both his integrity and the source of his revitalized poetic vision. Self-sacrifice and self-esteem went hand in hand, although this tandem of selflessness and egotism was an inevitably demanding one. His self-regard remained uncertain, given his dismay towards the Empire's longevity, his inability to bring some works to completion, his resurgent libido and his gradual abandonment by his family. Exile would test not only the patience of those closest to him but also his own resolve.

1852–5: From Brussels to Jersey

He spent the first eight months of exile in Brussels with other political refugees like the abolitionist Victor Schoelcher. Fearful that his revenue would be confiscated after his expulsion became official on 9 January, Hugo sold his shares and reinvested the money in new holdings and bonds in Brussels and London. He instructed his wife to auction their goods in the family home in Paris and to dissuade a headstrong Léonie from trying to follow him. Although he would continue to provide Léonie with financial support, he did not envisage a future for their affair. Hugo made it clear to Adèle that this reset would not include Juliette. Juliette was living with her maid on the other side of the Grand-Place in Brussels and helping him establish a regular pattern of work. He hoped that this routine would settle the debt-ridden Charles when he joined him after his release from prison. Hugo was keen on living a modest lifestyle in exile, both as an example to his 25-year-old son and, moreover, as a symbol of propriety that would stand in contrast to France's new leader.

Louis-Napoleon also moved quickly to adapt to his change in circumstance. A new constitution would enable him to proclaim the Second Empire by the end of 1852. The soon-to-be Napoleon III underpinned his widespread support for the imperial restoration with a loyal army, ever-present police force and powerful state bureaucracy. Censorship and the judiciary system silenced any republican or royalist opposition in the name of public order, and some 6,000 people were imprisoned or deported. Many more fled into exile. The regime looked to depoliticize the public by fostering economic growth and urban development, including Baron Haussmann's renovation of Paris which began the following year, and by adopting a popular foreign policy, which saw France victoriously ally with the British and Ottoman Empires during the mid-1850s to defeat the Russian tsar in the Crimean War. The Empire would very slowly move from authoritarianism to a more liberal position once its power was consolidated and would bring new prosperity to French society by doubling its overseas territories and by modernizing agriculture, transport and finance.[8]

For Hugo, however, there could be no atonement for how the would-be emperor had taken power. By the end of May, he had completed *Napoléon le Petit*, which was to be published by fellow exile Pierre-Jules Hetzel. It deployed quick-fire prose in a pamphlet format that pulled no punches on either Louis-Napoleon or his supporters. 'My God,' he complained, 'have we already reached that point when it's necessary to remind ourselves where this government came from?!' The final part proposed reforms to prevent a similar coup from occurring again, such as decentralizing power and separating Church and State, but there was no doubt that Hugo's hand had been motivated more by outrage than by optimism. 'Louis Bonaparte is perjury incarnate, felony in flesh and bone.'[9] Extracts appeared in newspapers from the Americas to Asia, and the first run of over 8,000 copies sold out.

Just before its publication on 7 August, Hugo relocated to Jersey, where his family reunited, minus François-Victor, who would join them later that year after serving his prison sentence. Hugo chose the island for its proximity to France and its long history of welcoming French exiles, as well as the Napoleonic overtones of banishment amidst the waves.[10] He knew he could not remain in Brussels since Belgian ministers were keen not to rile their neighbours, but he had no desire to go to London either. His arrival on Jersey was greeted by a welcoming party, including the Société Fraternelle of European exiles. The family soon moved into Marine Terrace, a large house by the sea in Saint Helier's suburbs; Juliette found an apartment in town.

Napoléon le Petit was only the first attack. 'The emperor is cooked on one side,' Hugo wryly told Hetzel, so it was time 'to flip him on the grill'[11] – or, more caustically, 'Since this fraud has two cheeks, I have to slap him twice.'[12] He was now writing poetry at ease. His estimates to Hetzel for the collection's size doubled within a month that winter to 3,000 verses. Nearly a year later in 1853, Hetzel ran a clandestine publication campaign in Brussels to ensure that this provocative new work outwitted police surveillance. The title wavered between *The Avenging Furies*, *Avenger's Song* and *Vengeful Rhymes*, among others, before being finalized as *Châtiments* (Chastisements, although 'thrashings' better evokes the vehemence of the French). Shifting from vengeance to admonition, Hugo wanted these poems to be read as a moral intervention rather than a personal vendetta. They were sardonic but written as a forecast of history's inescapable judgement.

Hugo's castigations conserved their satirical bite through a variety of forms, from lyric and epic to dialogues and meditations, through which Napoleon III took on different guises, such as despot, brute and sideshow act. Opening with the funereal 'Nox' to recall the coup, it progressed through seven parts, each borrowing the Second Empire's own rhetoric to undercut its authority. Titles like 'Society is Saved' and 'Order is Restored' introduced nearly a hundred poems that scorched the imperial veneer to reveal a morally bankrupt regime that was unworthy of France's history. He recounted his emotional meeting with the distraught grandmother of the young boy whose skull 'was cracked open like bark split on the trunk' by gunfire, citing the politics practised by 'Monsieur Napoleon' as the culprit: 'That is the reason why elderly grandmothers,/ With their poor greying fingers ravaged by the cold,/ Sew the shrouds of children who are seven years old.'[13] Generals, judges, priests and politicians were subsequently named and shamed, their reputations seared by his poems' red-hot branding irons.

His righteous power was drawn not from the laws of man, but from a divine order that brought light upon darkness. In the three hundred-line epic 'The Expiation', the rivalry between poet and emperor revealed history's much larger struggle between right and wrong. The first Napoleon repeatedly asks God if his defeats and exile were a form of punishment. He is told 'no'. It is only in his tomb that the fallen emperor is awoken to be shown the true punishment for his coup of 1799: his nephew's hijacking of the imperial legacy. 'You are their captive now! Their squalid paws/ Grip your bronze toes!'[14] By the end of the book, this hyperbolic antithesis between past glory and present disgrace has metamorphosed into the yet greater contrast between the bleakness of 'Nox' and the closing lustre of 'Lux', in which the poet foresees a bright new dawn free from tyranny. Having likened himself to prophets like Isaiah and John (who wrote the Book of Revelation in exile on the island of Patmos), Hugo married republicanism with spirituality to clip the wings of the imperial eagle. The casting of Napoleon I's own coup as worthy of retribution underlined that Hugo's faith in the future now rested with the people rather than with grandiose leaders, as it had done in his youth.

Hugo's self-fashioning as the arbiter of moral justice did not take the form of words alone. The daguerreotype had been patented fourteen years earlier, and Hugo had been persuaded of its superiority over lithographic production. Within months of arriving at Marine Terrace he had installed a studio. Photography offered Charles a pastime that he shared with his brother-in-law Vacquerie, but it was also a promising medium through which his father broadened his self-expression. Although Hugo never stepped behind the camera, he acted as an artistic director, encouraging the play of heavy contrasts and uneven lines, in addition to sending his son to Caen in May 1853 to train with the photographer Edmond Bacot. That summer, he announced his plans for a book of texts and photographs entitled *Jersey and the Channel Islands*, but the publication of *Châtiments* made publishers nervous, so the images were circulated instead among friends.

More would follow, for example when Bacot visited the Hugos in 1862, and these images would establish the importance of photography to Hugo's public persona. The Jersey period alone produced around 350 negatives capturing the family and their surroundings. Over sixty of these were portraits of Hugo, which three years later would appear in Vacquerie's book *Profiles and Grimaces* and in his illustrated copies of *Contemplations*. Hugo had three favoured poses: the reflective poet, with his hand to his forehead; the defiant republican, arms crossed and face tensed; and the stoic exile, slipping his hand into his coat and taken in profile. Photographs of him alone atop a coastline rock or 'listening to God' with his eyes closed were essential to the self-image that he wanted to project in the poems that he was now writing.[15] His interest in photography reflected other poetic concerns too, given the medium's ability to halt time and to lend figurative presence to past moments or absent exiles.

While in Jersey Hugo found another means of communing with that which was lost. During a visit in September 1853, which coincided with the anniversary of Léopoldine's death, family friend Delphine de Girardin introduced the Hugos to table-tapping, whereby spirits communicated with the living through a table. It had become a fashionable recreation in Paris thanks to the mid-century popularity of spiritualism on both sides of the Atlantic. The appeal of these seances was considerable. Adèle and the children, who enjoyed their lengthy conversation evenings with friends but missed Paris, welcomed a new source of excitement. At a time when he could no longer visit his daughter's grave, Hugo remained fascinated by spirituality for both its poetic and political significance in challenging empirical reason and evoking the solidarity of all life. He had also read widely around occultism and the relationship between an eternal source of creation and its mortal forms. He was familiar with elements of Jewish mysticism thanks to his acquaintance with Alexandre Weill since the late 1830s, and in exile had been reading about the Hindu doctrine of reincarnation.[16] Local folklore further nurtured these interests in the transmigration of souls. Jersey's Neolithic dolmens and its supposed ghosts all caught Hugo's attention,

Charles Hugo, *Victor Hugo on the Rock of Exiles*, Jersey, 1853.

Auguste Vacquerie, *Victor Hugo Listening to God*, 1853.

one of which – the White Lady – supposedly made direct contact in Marine Terrace.

For the next two years the family communed with over one hundred souls. Léopoldine was the first, which guaranteed her loved ones' willingness to persist with contacting the dead. Using Charles as the primary medium at a small three-legged table, conversations with Isaiah, the prophet Muhammad and Shakespeare, to name a few, were transcribed in verse or prose. All these spirits conveniently spoke French. The conspicuously Hugolian character to the writing alone calls into question their messages, as does the transcripts' tendency to manifest the subconscious desires of the participants and to flatter Hugo's ego. In several seances, Jesus criticized Jersey's Druid history and Christianity, and called for prophets of a new religion, much as Hugo's poetry advocated.

The credibility of these conversations is beside the point. What mattered was Hugo's belief in these spirits' existence and the affinity he played on between being ('être') and spirit ('spectre'). The transcriptions can be read similarly to surrealist automatism or therapeutic psychography: as a method of exploring the mind by giving it autonomy.[17] These communions permitted his impressionable imagination to apprehend a spirit world through which the impermanence of time could be rethought as an eternal life force. They formed the strangest addition to the eclectic evolution of his thinking but were far from being parlour games. Spiritism nourished his ideas about the reckoning of good and evil across the ages. They also fed his productivity, and he composed over two hundred poems in eighteen months. 'I'm drifting across poetry's open seas,' he beamed.[18] *Les Misérables* (the updated title for *Les Misères*) would have to wait, despite Hetzel's entreaties, and in July 1854 Hugo signed a contract for a new volume, *Contemplations*.

The table-tapping came to an end in September 1855. A young participant, Jules Allix, suffered a nervous breakdown, reminding

Photograph by Henry Mullins of Victor Hugo (right) with his sons Charles (left) and François-Victor (centre), 1860.

Hugo of Eugène and the potential cost of forsaking reason for vision. The world of the living was also pressing in. Hugo had kept his distance from the infighting of the Société Fraternelle but had been unable to remain silent on Britain's alliance with France in the Crimean War. In June 1855, he found the words 'Hugo is a bad man' scrawled on his front door and was hit on

Photograph by Charles Hugo of Adèle Hugo (left) with her parents, *c.* 1853–5.

the head by a rock while out walking. That autumn, the exiles'
newspaper *L'Homme* published a scathing co-signed letter that
questioned Queen Victoria as both a monarch and a woman for
allying with Napoleon III. Hugo found the letter to be in poor taste,
but he openly declared solidarity with the paper's staff, who were
now banned from the island. He chose to leave Jersey before his
own expulsion was inevitably ordered. The family and Juliette
were to be uprooted once again. The crossing to the smaller island

Photograph by Auguste Vacquerie of the Hugo family in Guernsey, *c.* 1855–6.
From left to right: Charles, his sister Adèle behind him, their mother,
François-Victor behind her and his father in profile.

of Guernsey on 31 October was rough but the welcome was
warm, as were the supportive protests on the British mainland
throughout November.

1856–61: The Poet's Pinnacle

If *Châtiments* was akin to Hugo cleansing the muck from his shoes
as he crossed a new threshold, *Contemplations* was the sign of a poet
hitting his stride. His most ambitious volume of poetry yet was a
runaway success. Published in the spring of 1856 in Paris and in
Brussels, its outwardly apolitical content prompted no ban from
the Empire or its neighbours. *Contemplations* contained 158 poems,
mostly written since the early 1840s but some dating back a decade
earlier and organized within two volumes – 'Once' and 'Today'.
The first reflected on the years up to Léopoldine's death in 1843;
the second detailed the poet's grief before tracking his recovery and
the new sense of life's mysteries that he attained. A philosopher's
demanding curiosity moves both volumes forward, asking why life's
pleasures must be matched by its sorrows, and meditating on the
universe's intentions. He looked outwards across the cosmos itself
to understand his experiences within a vast symbiosis of all things.
Death thereby revealed itself as part of a never-ending creation,
turning 'Thrones into gallows, gallows into thrones,/ Maternal eyes
to fountains, gold to grime.'[19] With his daughter's grave separating
the two volumes, he presented death as a pivotal moment in a
continuum rather than a conclusive endpoint in order to contemplate
a universal divine force.

He had altered various composition dates and ordered his poems
psychologically rather than chronologically, but not to be deceitful.
On the contrary, he introduced a progression of his emotions that
was in sync with this idea of life as proliferation. He wanted to
consider all of existence through his single life story, or what the

short preface called 'the memoirs of a soul'. He promised to take his reader from cradle to grave through youth, illusion and despair to the brink of the infinite. The preface's imagery of life as a stream pouring into the soul was strengthened by internal rhythms and generated a key metaphor: that of *Contemplations* as a reflective element or surface. 'Take this mirror and look at yourself in it . . . When I talk to you about myself, I am talking about you.' His visions could only have relevance through this awareness of unity: '[We] are the same teardrop falling from the same eye.'[20]

Hugo relied on the public and private sides of himself to lend both substance and impetus to his reflections. Poems such as 'Reply to a Bill of Indictment' portrayed the rebellious writer who 'trampled good taste and ye olde ffrenche verse' and 'dressed the old dictionary in liberty's colours'.[21] Others delved into his more intimate self, such as 'While Knocking on a Door', in which he mulls over the loss of his parents, brothers and first two children. The most recited of these verses is the well-known 'At dawn tomorrow . . .' – a staple of French literary education. This short poem recounts the poet's journey to his daughter's grave. He finds repose and contentment back at her side, as conveyed by the final verse's identical rhyme schemes and the burst of colour from the golden sunset, flowering heather and spray of holly. Through his recollections, he did not seek closure to his grief, but to integrate that pain into a more inclusive view of what life was.

This integration of disbelief and faith was revelatory for his spiritual journey, making the book into a religious text of sorts. This personal scripture was more secular than the Christian royalist verse of his youth and more arbitrary through its melange of sources. It interlaced the mystical aspects of European Romanticism and world religions like Christianity with various rational methods, from ancient Greek philosophy to the Saint-Simonian humanitarianism of his own century. His beliefs depended on a munificent deity as the source and essence of all life, whose perfection was unimaginable in mortal form and whose light shone so intensely that no human eyes could measure its endless expanse.

The majority of the book's antitheses draw on the contrast between light and darkness. This divine light was neither the God of Christian doctrine nor that of eighteenth-century deism, both of which had been re-appropriated by Hugo. Reason and moral sentiment offered partial ways of knowing God, but the imperfections of mortality prevented human beings from acquiring a complete knowledge. Sensing the divine's boundless power in all creation allowed God to be known in this incomplete but truthful way. Life was not confined to the organic matter of nature but spread out across the universe, whether in the stones beneath the poet's feet or in the gigantic stars over his head, which were themselves but 'pebbles seen in the dim sepulcher'.[22] Everything therefore spoke in an endless dialogue that the poet could hear.

At the end of the first volume, Hugo articulated this metaphysics in one of his lengthiest contemplations, 'Magnitudo Parvi' ('The Greatness of Small Things'). Walking with his daughter at nightfall, he reads the 'black book of the sky' and marvels at how all elements of creation are on a par with one another, no matter what their size or place. The twin flickers on the horizon of a shepherd's fire and a shining star pull his gaze in opposite directions to the earthly and the cosmic. Across this ever-widening expanse he feels 'the hurricane of being' and 'the eternal spray of Creation's ocean'. This all-embracing motion demands more dynamic perspectives than simple sight affords. The poem's heterometric structure invokes the shifting unities of what he sees, and the language kindles an animated but captivating vision. Uncommon plurals ('Babels of stars rising into the Babylons of night'); oxymoron ('Dream World! Real Ideal!'); juxtaposition ('Sublime radiance or hideous blaze!'); totalization (man's solitude is both ravine and mountain); anthropomorphic constructions (living shadows, screaming rocks, singing fires) – all evoke a mysterious cosmos imbued with life.

'Magnitudo Parvi' anticipated the final section of the second volume, where Hugo set his ongoing commitment to art's illuminating effects within this context of metempsychosis. Two other hefty works – 'The Magi' and 'What the Mouth of the Shadows Says' – help round off the book by elaborating upon the poet's duty to foster a literacy of the universe as 'the bible of trees, mountains, and waters', and by stressing the moral importance of his theology. The first poem's title recalled one of the oldest monotheistic religions, Zoroastrianism, whose Magi believed in a compassionate creator and in free will, and the Wise Men of the Bible who visited Jesus. Hugo lauded the imagination's openness as the only ritual required of true priesthood, in which minds became conduits between the divine and its material, temporal creation as a space of constant becoming. From Ariosto to Zarathustra, and whether Primaticcio in art or Pythagoras in philosophy, each saw the 'vastnesses' of eternity and pushed at the banks of human knowledge to allow 'a sort of fluid God' to flow more freely into civilization. This fluidity explains *Contemplations*' overall fascination with energy flows like wind, tides and electricity, and its imagining of life's origins as an unconstrained and uncoordinated event, not dissimilar to the twentieth century's Big Bang theory.[23]

In the second poem, he emphasized the moral implications of this sentient cosmos. In a universe where life and death are inseparable, the soul dissipates along an immense scale of being when the body expires. It either comes closer towards the light or drifts further into darkness depending on how much it has accepted or abused life's interconnected nature. The more love that the soul emits and the greater its sense of equality between all life, the more the divine is apparent; the more the soul resists this light, the more obliterated it risks becoming. Darker hearts disband into men's spittle (Judas), the mountain face (Nimrod) and the hearth's flames (Nero). Only compassion brings redemption, thus Hugo implored his reader to respect all life, be it saint or

slug, and to intuit the sorrow that resonated in everything from
the executioner's block to the natural elements. Crucially, the
responsibility was ours alone. Human fate was not pre-determined
by God, as the divine was not immediately evident in this self-
governing world. Instead, 'all beings are their own scales' and must
find their own way. 'Free, man knows where goodness ends, where
evil begins . . . Relight the extinguished soul!'[24] As in *Châtiments*, the
end is hopeful, sounded by an angel's final exclamation: 'Beginning!'

It proved to be less a suggestive last word than a promise, because
the Gospel according to Victor Hugo was only just getting under way:
'I believe that Christianity has had its time. Even Luther's robes are
too tight for sons of the Revolution.'[25] Over the next six years he
would add to its heft further still. *The Legend of the Ages* turned his
spiritual viewpoints on to humankind's unsteady progress, from
Eden and Rome via Christianity, Islam and paganism through to the
Renaissance and 1789. The preface explained that this book would
'depict the human race, simultaneously and successively, in all
its aspects – history, fable, philosophy, religion, science – which
comprise one vast ascension toward the light'.[26] His plan was to
supplement this epic with two similarly colossal volumes of poetry
that he had started on Jersey. By considering wickedness and infinite
grace through its two antithetical protagonists, *The End of Satan* and
God delved further into the moral and religious frames of reference
for *The Legend of the Ages* and again signalled Hugo's high regard for
Dante and Milton. In *The End of Satan*, the fallen Lucifer inspires
cruelty in humankind via his daughter, Lilith. God, however, has
created another daughter from Satan's wing, the angel Liberty, who
eventually saves her father from his cold, sunless abyss to redeem
humanity. *God* developed the image of a deity who eludes the
human ability to comprehend or represent its dominion. The poet
assiduously but vainly tries to break through the limitations of his
knowledge and to bring some kind of plenitude to the vacant ellipses
at the beginning and end of his enquiry.

Only *The Legend of the Ages* would be published during Hugo's lifetime, in the autumn of 1859, followed by two further instalments in 1877 and 1883. Critics thought it was less accessible than *Contemplations*, but its poetic ambition and storyteller's confidence attracted a wide audience. Neither *The End of Satan* nor *God* were completed and would only appear posthumously. One reason for this was the arduous demands they made on Hugo. Like *The Legend of the Ages*, they packed burly alexandrines, encyclopaedic erudition and mystic visions onto their superabundant pages. Furthermore, each one amplified the more esoteric tones of Hugo's voice, although the prospective status of *God* lends itself well to the volume's evocation of an unknowable divine:

> Just when ideas open, words deform them.
> How can the face of the deep be represented,
> The shape of boundless life, the attitude
> Of fullness and omnipotence?[27]

What was also apparent was that these collections were not fulfilling one of the objectives from *The Legend of the Ages*, which was to celebrate the nineteenth century as history's transformation into a harmonious future. *The Legend of the Ages* conspicuously jumped over the French Revolution towards a twentieth century free from tyranny, scarcity and superstition. *The End of Satan* was supposed to conclude with Liberty's destruction of the Bastille in 1789 for Lucifer's pardon, but Hugo tellingly never managed to write this section. In both cases, his approach to the Revolution as the clear-cut beginning of an end to humanity's ills bordered on the evangelical. Each instance was made all the less convincing by these books' extensive coverage of human progress as a troubled rather than direct march through a history in which the divine was unattainable. Whatever their difficulties, these three collections sustained a creative flurry in their miscellany of spiritualism, history and fantasy.

Such was this creativity's dynamism that it exceeded the written word. The sizeable revenue from *Contemplations* gave Hugo a new page on which to write: he bought a large townhouse in St Peter Port, which he christened Hauteville House. No. 38 Hauteville was larger than the property he had been renting and boasted a much bigger garden overlooking the sea. His love of a thriving garden had deepened on Jersey with the input of a fellow green-fingered exile, Adolphe Le Flô. Another of Hugo's loves would be close by: Juliette found a small house from which she could see her poet on the upper balcony (as would passers-by when he took one of his brisk outdoor

The rear of Hauteville House, Guernsey, 2017. The glass lookout that Hugo had constructed as a work space can be seen atop the house to the right.

The dining room in Hauteville House, with tapestry on the ceiling and ceramic tiles around the fireplace; photograph by T. B. Banks & Co., *c.* 1900. Latin inscriptions are carved into the panelling around the room, including 'absentes adsunt' (those absent are present) and 'Ego Hugo' (I Hugo).

wash-downs). His statement that 'the house comes entirely out of *Contemplations*' acknowledged more than just a financial debt.[28] The house became a poem in its own right – 'a veritable three-storey autograph', according to Charles, written in fabrics, carpentry, ceramics and glasswork.[29] Hugo commissioned local artisans to implement his plans for his architectural tercet and, with Juliette's help, raided the island's bric-a-brac traders and antique stores for fittings and furnishings.

Once it was finished in the early 1860s, Hauteville House was a monument to Hugo's tastes for innovative ways of seeing and being, which can be enjoyed today on guided museum tours. Modern gas lighting dressed a space that was as carefully thought through as any of the sets for Hugo's dramas. The bottoms of glass bottles were patterned into wooden transom windows in the hallway, as if opening multiple eyes onto the visitor while liquefying the space above their head. Ceilings merged into walls in the tapestry lounge, where fabric spread out above and around the central table (itself a repurposed door), and in the passageway alongside the dining room, where plates were arranged overhead as well as on the usual side shelves. The dining room displayed engraved writing on the walls, a forever empty chair for absent souls that was set in between the garden windows, and a superimposed double 'H' made of several dozen individual tiles, through which the first letter of the family name and the house's initials folded together. The invitation to read the house continued on the upper floors with a mix of Renaissance, Gothic and Orientalist styles. One of numerous Latin inscriptions – 'Nox, Mors, Lux' (Night, Death, Light) – alerted visitors to Hugo's belief that light and freedom could only be attained through darkness and struggle. That trajectory was mirrored by the climb from the shadowy main hallway up the staircase, which was illuminated by an oval skylight. In addition,

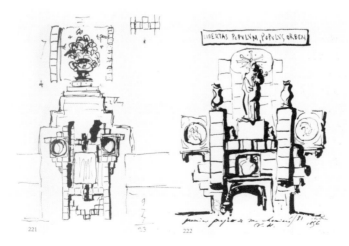

Hugo's design for the ceramic fireplace. The double 'H' can also be read as a rebuff to Louis-Napoleon's tendency to imprint his own initials on public spaces.

Victor Hugo, *Souvenir of a Castle in the Vosges*, 1857, pen and brown ink wash, gouache and pochoir. A jagged, unclear castle breaks through a sepia fog, evoking the opaque character of memory.

a glass 'lookout' was constructed atop the house, from where he would be able to see the French coastline on a clear day and observe the tides while working.

The visual and spatial imagination that had shaped Hauteville House also found a rich outlet in Hugo's artworks. He had drawn since his youth and had produced caricatures and sketches of his travels for his family. On calling cards for friends, he projected his name or initials cutting across the page in decorative but irregular fonts that played with art's traditions of signature. As his conception of poetic *voyance* evolved, his style became more contemplative. He worked only on paper, and mostly on a small scale in pen-and-ink washes. Landscapes and outlines shimmered and melted in pieces that revelled in brightness and shadow. In their dense emphasis on contrast and abstraction over colour and form, these works visualized a mind moving back and forth between materiality and mood. Even his more representational drawings such as *The Hanged Man*, which was created to focus his indignation at an Englishman's fumbled execution in 1854, defamiliarized the visual field with a

Victor Hugo, *Town on a Plain*, date unknown, ink wash, watercolour and gouache. Hugo's playful signature is larger than the town on the horizon, implying that his sense of self foregrounds his ability to see and represent.

Victor Hugo, *Landscape with Three Trees*, 1850, pen, ink wash and pencil. This chiaroscuro work recalls Rembrandt's famous 1643 etching of the same name.

faceless but recognizably human body suspended between a penetrating light above and an all-consuming blackness below.

He was highly experimental in exile, favouring imagery that took advantage of the unfinished nature of shapes and forms. These works enacted a world view that was immersed in the simultaneity of creation and erosion. Mixed with the standard materials of ink and graphite were perishable elements such as blackberry juice, coffee, ink-drenched strips of lace and soot. He used the point of his quill to draw and the hairs to paint, sometimes with his eyes closed and using his left rather than preferred right hand to let his unconscious mind take control. He also achieved this effect by using processes that are more readily associated with twentieth-century practices, such as stencils in which a castle's presence depended on (and could be reconfigured through) its absence, and symmetrical compositions that anticipated

Paul Chenay, *John Brown*, 1860: an engraving of Victor Hugo's *'Ecce Lex'* (Behold the Law), or *The Hanged Man* (1854), pen and brown ink wash over graphite pencil, black ink and charcoal. Hugo's drawing protesting the hanging of an Englishman on Guernsey in 1854 was later engraved by Chenay following the execution of the American abolitionist John Brown. Chenay was married to Adèle Hugo's younger sister, Julie.

Victor Hugo, *Lace and Spectres*, c. 1855–6, ink, lace and charcoal. Dipping the lace in ink before pressing it onto the paper and adding fresh touches, Hugo played with the amorphous qualities of his patterned material. Various influences are at work, including the 'blottesque' techniques of Alexander Cozens and John Constable, and the 19th century's occultist fascination with the unconscious.

Hermann Rorschach's inkblots. His drawings were mostly for private enjoyment among his friends and supporters, and they were much less well known than his writing during his lifetime. The first exhibition was only organized three years after his death in Paris by Meurice, after which Vincent Van Gogh would refer to the works as 'astonishing things'.[30]

Hauteville House itself became the easel for another kind of self-fulfilment thanks to the location of Hugo's bedroom, which was tucked away in the attic workspace with easy access to the domestic staff's quarters. His private diary used coded notations to itemize his sexual activities, which he seems to have enjoyed mainly with the house's chambermaids and almost certainly beyond its walls also, with Guernsey's prostitutes. The pleasures (perhaps fantasies) of sight and touch continued to intoxicate him. At the same time, he took a clear interest in the lives of a number of the women in his diary and offered them gifts such as winter fuel and extra clothing. His generous but discreet expenditure might be understood as both courtesy and penance from a republican who believed in women's rights to suffrage, education and employment, and in what he saw as the human right to sexual liberation and free love. His infatuation with the female body did not give rise to misogyny or violence, nor did it deflate his commitment to equality. His poem honouring the socialist Pauline Roland in *Châtiments*, and 'Melancholia' from *Contemplations*, which scorned society's apathy towards exploited women, reiterated his determination that

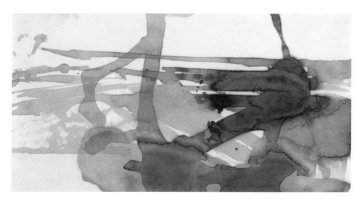

Abstract ink composition by Victor Hugo, *c.* 1864–9. Shapes overlap and bleed into one another, lending depth and movement to a shimmering inkscape where forms emerge and retreat.

Victor Hugo, *Cut paper with a cross (study for Léopoldine's tomb)*, *c*. 1858, ink and stencil. A hand reaching into the darkness, or a monster devouring the light? Hugo's use of stencilling and cut-outs allowed him to entertain multiple possibilities at once.

women be freed from economic coercion and granted the same social and legal footing as men.

The heavily suggestive nature of the diary's encryptions weakens the theory that Hugo used code simply to protect himself from discovery, especially given that he would donate every page and sheet of his writing to the Bibliothèque nationale de France upon his death. His coded language shows that, even in his intimate moments, his imagination was active. Women's names were hidden within and between other words, and their bodies became geographical formations. The human and natural worlds blended: 'Switzerland' could be deciphered to signify breasts (peaks and milk), for example, and references to forests and ravines were just as erotic. His words and actions pointed to a universe that was not only sentient but sensual in its surge of life. Since the insatiable creation describedin the theology of *Contemplations* was fundamentally loving, it could also be forever passionate: 'And amorous life overwhelmed/ The fields, the rocks, the capes, the world/ With the ocean's monstrous sperm.'[31]

In the eighth section of *The Legend of the Ages*, he had heavily eroticized all of existence when recounting the fate of a satyr at the foot of Mount Olympus. The satyr's Dionysiac and priapic image in Greek mythology, as well as his hybrid human and equine features, made him an ideal figure for Hugo's Romantic pantheism. The satyr's excitement towards everything around him, from women to flora to the very breeze itself, dishevels the forest and displeases the gods. His song becomes increasingly breathless as it summons nature's splendour: 'Make way, for I am Pan! On your knees, Jupiter!'[32] As the god of the wild, Pan's orgiastic acts of natural propagation overpower the dogmatic Olympus and support Hugo's contention that faith needed to rid itself of hierarchical institutions to find God.

It would nonetheless be misleading to claim that Hugo was comfortable with such widespread arousal. It is true that his gleeful excess when liberating himself from social mores is recognizable in his diary, along with his theatrical liking for secrets known only to the privileged audience. That same obsessive bookkeeping hints at a more anxious attitude, however, and a desire to bridle his urges by delineating periods of restraint, with an eye to making those examples of self-control last longer.[33] These tensions are at play in *The End of Satan*, which is after all preoccupied with the Bible's archetypal guilty exile. His inability to complete his fable betrayed a lack of conviction in resolving the dissident angel's egomania. Conversely, his return to the manuscript at the turn of the decade after the initial writing phase on Jersey was symptomatic of a yearning to find some release from self-indulgence through a purer, more transcendent love. Such a longing had, in effect, minimized his physicality with Juliette. Their relationship was now much less an expression of carnal desire than it was of deeply tender devotion. 'Often, you give your heart, but we take only your body,' he later lamented about men's love of women.[34] His diary also indicates that his sexual whims slowed or stopped during concentrated periods of writing but intensified at times of strife, suggesting that orgasm was as much an addictive analgesic as a stimulant. His ambivalent relationship to his sexuality was evidently not getting easier, even as it continued to fertilize his literary creativity.

Napoleon III's announcement in August 1859 of a full amnesty for exiles was met with a stern public response from Hugo just two days later: 'When liberty returns, I will return.'[35] Not everyone shared his dedication to the cause, however. Several friends announced that they would accept the amnesty. Hugo knew that his family wanted to go back to France as well, having grown tired of island life. His wife and daughter had already spent four months in Paris as Adèle senior was concerned about Adèle junior's increasingly withdrawn behaviour and bouts of psychosomatic illness. Juliette helped to counteract his feelings of desertion and had at last come to know his sons. Hauteville House's numerous visitors also brought him comfort, as did its growing menagerie of dogs, cats, chickens and fish. But Madame Hugo would herself start spending more months away from Guernsey, followed later by Charles.

The exiled patriot and the abandoned patriarch had renewed incentive to revisit the novel that he had left in limbo in 1848. With a more developed sense of the spiritual value to his endeavours, a story about the social and moral importance of self-sacrifice had become especially meaningful. That impetus was made all the stronger for the ageing Romantic by a reminder of his mortality. In the summer of 1858, he had been diagnosed with a potentially fatal anthrax infection. He took over three months to heal and had modified his preferred exercise routine of swimming in the sea. His hair was greying. Time was catching up with him.

Hugo also knew that his voice carried further than ever before in a global literary market of ever-growing audiences. Industrialization had reduced printing costs and opened more efficient routes of supply by railway and steamship, while improvements to education were dramatically raising literacy rates. In addition, Hugo's name commanded attention thanks to his camaraderie with the international republican community. Exile was a 'common homeland' for those seeking a universal republic, as he told the Russian activist Alexander Herzen,[36] hence the donations Hugo made to relief funds for exiles in London and Brussels. He was also responsive to invitations to lend his voice where needed, such as Giuseppe Mazzini's call for support in the Italian unification movement in 1856.

One of his career's most famous interventions looked to an already established republic. In a letter to the United States of America in the international press on 2 December 1859 (a date with ominous political significance for any French exile), he pleaded for the life of the abolitionist John Brown. Brown had been sentenced to death for trying to incite an armed slave revolt in West Virginia. Hugo dodged the thornier questions of political violence to concentrate on the root issue, warning that the execution would mark a moral point of no return. 'Let America know and think about this: there is something more frightening than Cain killing Abel, and that is Washington killing Spartacus.'[37] To the public's knowledge, Brown's hanging had been postponed from 2 December to 16 December, whereas in actuality he was executed that same day. The letter's timing heightened its pathos – and its author's celebrity in North America – at an emotionally charged moment. The contentious debate over slavery would push the country into civil war just over sixteen months later.

Brown's execution was disconcerting to Hugo. A free republic had killed a freedom fighter, making this controversy one that he could not easily let be. His argument in early 1860 to a Haitian newspaper editor was both strong willed and prophetic: the Union was broken, but the Southern States had signed slavery's death warrant by executing Brown, and Haiti's 'great example' proved that black hands were helping to light this path to progress.[38] Early in 1861, he allowed engraved reproductions of *The Hanged Man* to be published along with a new letter, forever associating the image with freedom's ultimate sacrifice and Christ-like martyrdom. In a letter to the Guadeloupian abolitionist Octave Giraud the following year, he likened slavery to an ulcer that needed to be removed from the American republic's face. John Brown had resurrected *Bug-Jargal*.

Propelled by his sense of public responsibility, Hugo dug out the manuscript of *Les Misérables* in late April 1860, which Juliette had safeguarded along with his other work. Over the next fourteen months, he worked on bringing his novel to the altitudes that his mind had reached in exile. A bout of laryngitis in December reminded him that there was no time to lose. He grew his iconic beard as a protection against future illness and took the first of his annual summer vacations in exile, following doctors' advice that he finally enjoy some time away. Before going to Holland, he and Juliette travelled to Belgium to visit the site of the Battle of

Waterloo, which had become integral to the book's understanding of nineteenth-century history. The novel had become enormous. Hugo enhanced multiple character arcs, enriched his use of symbols, and developed numerous narrative digressions that would occupy well over a quarter of the book. These digressions offered new vantage points for his reader to consider while also controlling the novel's pace. They utilized the poet-philosopher's ability to stockpile all manner of facts and opinions into thickset and often roving prose. Each digression allowed him to talk at length about subjects as varied as slang, convents and waste, and to maximize fiction's potential as a vehicle for discussion as much as entertainment.

During this revision process, a young Belgian called Albert Lacroix secured the publishing contract. Hugo had seen how lucrative the publishing industry had become in the success of novels like Sue's *Mysteries of Paris*, which had begun spawning a 'city mysteries' series, Dumas's *The Count of Monte Cristo* (1844), and Dickens' *A Tale of Two Cities* (1859), and he wanted enough money to guarantee his family's future. Lacroix industriously settled the contract Hugo had signed in the late 1840s by promising Gosselin's successor, Charles Pagnerre, exclusive French publishing rights, and he borrowed the necessary funds to meet Hugo's eye-watering price: 300,000 Francs for an eight-year licence and translation rights. It was the equivalent of the combined annual salaries of 120 civil servants – at least a couple of million pounds or several million dollars in today's currency – and was unrivalled by nineteenth-century standards. Lacroix put together a publicity campaign for a simultaneous launch across over a dozen international cities from St Petersburg to Rio de Janeiro, whetting the public appetite for what was billed as the novel of the century.

1862–70: *Perseverando*

When the first volumes appeared in April 1862, they swiftly sold out in Paris and went on to achieve immediate worldwide success.[39] Hugo was aggrieved by the relative silence of the liberal press, for whom the novel's spiritual elements proved difficult to accept when secularism featured so heavily in left-wing discourse. He correctly predicted, however, that right-wing commentators would disdain his sympathy for society's outcasts. He also knew that his unapologetically Romantic style rejected the Realist vogue for tighter plotting and more sober narration. But *Les Misérables* had been written for a popular rather than critical audience. Categorical world views like atheistic materialism or dogmatic morality had no place in his thinking, any more than literary fashions, since they limited what he wanted to say. Lacroix was certainly not the only promoter to realize that the story's appeal could be as considerable as its profit margins. *Les Misérables* was one of the most adapted novels in history even before its ever-popular musical version began conquering the world stage in the 1980s. Following in the novel's footsteps, *Les Miz* is a global phenomenon. It has played in over fifty countries and nearly 350 cities, connecting with audiences of all types and backgrounds.

Like *Contemplations*, *Les Misérables* is full of personal references yet universal in spirit. Dates, figures and spaces all tend to have biographical significance for Hugo – Valjean's prison number 24601 (signifying 24 June 1801, the date on which Hugo was conceived), the idyllic garden at the Rue Plumet (recalling the Feuillantines), the date of Cosette's wedding in 1833 (Hugo's anniversary with Juliette) and so on. Elements of one life are recycled into a book about everything for everyone: 'a vast mirror reflecting humankind in action at one given moment'.[40] The action unfolds between 1815 and 1833 but looks back in time and forward to a new century to release the events into the flow of history. Along this current, one

The preface from Hugo's original manuscript of *Les Misérables*. The page illustrates his usual technique of editing his work: he would fold over the left-hand side while writing on the right, then unfold the paper and add in any corrections.

Frenchman's journey from the *bagne* in Toulon to the streets of Paris during the Restoration contains truths for all readers. A single-sentence preface locates this expansive field of vision. Shortages of work, food and education are seen within a broader view of 'ignorance and misery'.

The title allowed Hugo to signpost this relationship between the material and moral levels of social reality. *Misére* denotes both abject poverty and moral wretchedness, making it difficult for translators to abandon Hugo's French title. The change of title from the concept ('misère') to the people who experience it (the 'misérables') reinforced the novel's human dimensions while preserving the double meaning. This hedging was important, since society's poor were easily vilified as what Edmund Burke in 1790 had notoriously called 'the swinish multitude'. It was easier to dehumanize this underclass by naturalizing the association of poverty and immorality than it was to address the social deficiencies that created such scarcity of resource and conscience in the first place. The narrator is adamant that 'society must look these issues in the face, since it is society that produces them'.[41] Poverty is not a measure of individual value. Likewise, Fantine's abandonment by Cosette's father, Tholomyès, and Bamatabois' callous behaviour towards her in the snow disprove any assumption that wealth or social rank guarantee virtue. Defying such essentialism, Hugo argued that we are defined only by our choices.

One choice readers of *Les Misérables* often confess to is bypassing Hugo's digressions, which vary from momentary side-glances to nearly fifty pages in the case of his nineteen-chapter discussion of Waterloo. It is easy to wish Hugo would be quiet and get on with the story instead of letting his work become one of those 'large, loose, baggy monsters' of nineteenth-century fiction that Henry James fretted over.[42] The novel's melodrama engrosses its readers with memorable characters, embellished coincidences and thrilling scenes like the storming of the barricade on the Rue de la Chanvrerie and

Jean Valjean's escape through the Parisian sewers. But the digressions are a necessary part of his recuperative outlook. 'This book is a tragedy in which infinity plays the lead. Man plays a supporting role.'[43] The very idea of centres and margins is misleading, as is the distinction between progress and deviation. In the structural as well as metaphorical sense, the novel's heart is too big to be neatly contained in something as narrow or fixed as a central plot.

Fortunately, Hugo provided a fruitful way into his epic. In a major change from the earlier manuscript, the novel opens not with Jean Valjean's arrival in Digne after his release from prison, but with the story of the open-hearted Bishop Myriel in 'A Just Man' (the first book of Part One). The narrator announces on the first page that the details about Myriel are themselves a digression from the story to come, obliging the reader to broaden their interest beyond the plot's ostensible core. This structural change prepares the reader for the later digressions by putting into practice the novel's overarching theme of restitution. It gets them to rethink the value of peripheral and supposedly inconsequential material as having an underlying connection to the central tale. As the catalyst for Jean Valjean's redemption, the bishop who rejects the material trappings of his post and treats all life as equal is pivotal to the novel's moral, historical and spiritual consciousness.

Myriel's story introduces Hugo's vision of a universe in which all things are bound together rather than ranked. He can be seen in contemplation in his garden at night, 'opening his soul . . . full of ecstasy in the middle of the universal radiance of creation'.[44] A true priest for Hugo, he needs no episcopal palace or opulent robes. The candlesticks he adds to Valjean's haul of stolen silver symbolically bring light into the ex-convict's dark soul and illuminate his difficult path forward. Similarly, 'A Just Man' lights the way for readers. This opening digression has its ethical corollary in the esteem that the novel has for France's allegedly negligible or worthless elements. Valjean has no noble blood or feats of military prowess to speak of;

the Paris insurrection of 1832 possesses nothing of the magnitude of the revolutions in 1789, 1830 and 1848; and the southern commune of Digne, the northern coastal town of Montreuil-sur-Mer and the workers' districts of Paris are a far cry from well-to-do society and the corridors of political power. But the people, episodes and places of *Les Misérables* show that the seemingly insignificant can be as illustrious as any of history's great motors.

The novel's interest in which forces truly shape the world converge around its principal human character, Jean Valjean. Imprisoned for stealing a loaf of bread to feed his sister and her children, Valjean's sentence was extended due to repeated escape attempts. Nineteen years of incarceration have left him embittered and ostracized, but Myriel's kindness spurs him to reinvent himself. Valjean's plight, both as a convict plunged into the abyss of the penal system and as a man finding his way towards new dawns, reveals the novel's idea of history as a tide of transformation. His chain is fastened on the same day that Napoleon's victory at Montenotte is proclaimed in 1796, only to be released in the same year as the emperor's fall at Waterloo. This inversion's significance becomes clear in the Waterloo digression, in which the battle becomes a re-enactment of the *Iliad*. It marks a historical turning point, when the Revolution's energy diverted from the military men of destiny such as Napoleon, who wanted to control fate, to those who were prepared to open their minds to a less servile, more independent reality. France's downfall is reconfigured as a new start for the Revolution, the harbingers of which will not be rulers dreaming of glory, but anyone prepared to move with history's indeterminate flux. If defeat's affinity with victory can be realized, then the future can remain free.

Taking the same road north from Toulon to Digne that Napoleon travelled before him, Valjean's suitability for this kind of citizenship is manifest in his increasingly self-determining and altruistic actions. His multiple roles (thief, prisoner, mayor, gardener, adoptive father, rescuer), his inventiveness (revitalizing the town of Montreuil-sur-Mer, repeatedly changing his identity, mastering the art of escape) and his struggles with his own conscience (sparing the innocent Champmathieu a prison sentence, forsaking revenge on his tormentor Javert, braving the barricades to save Cosette's suitor, Marius) all qualify him as the novel's exemplary *misérable*. His heroism is shored up by the antagonists Thénardier and Javert. The lawless Thénardier cravenly loots corpses on the Waterloo battlefield and in the Parisian sewers, and has no love for his children. Lacking in scruples, he typifies the self-interested greed that Hugo saw devouring society's moral instincts: 'I need money, I need a lot of money, I need an enormous amount of money!'[45] Javert also comes from society's underclass, having been born in prison. In contrast to Thénardier's violent materialism, he exudes the virtues of law and order, but unlike Valjean, his devotion to God has the blind conviction of a fanatic. He cannot make sense of either Valjean's mercy towards him or his own leniency in letting his prey go. 'Appalling! . . . infallibility is not infallible, the code does not have the last word, the law can be mistaken.'[46] Where Valjean is reborn thanks to Myriel's revelation of this sublime truth, Javert throws himself to his death.

Javert's fate should be enough to dissuade anyone from offering the final word about *Les Misérables*, but the novel has other warnings regarding complacency. At the very end, the reader is told that the natural elements have discoloured Valjean's gravestone and eroded the words that had been chalked on it: 'The thing just happened of its own accord,/ As night comes on when day is done.'[47] In its decay and its image of nature's cycles as the only true fate, the epitaph offers an ephemeral conclusion. Words can be written but are not permanent; openings and closures are perpetual. Valjean's sacrifices, like those of Marius' father, of Cosette's mother and of the fallen at the barricade, provide only the hope of a better world rather than its certainty, especially since Thénardier has become a slave trader in

Photograph by Henry Blackwell Frankland of Hugo hosting local children from poor families at Hauteville House, February 1868.

America. Left with this ending, it is difficult not to wonder how Marius and Cosette – the newly-wed inheritors of Valjean's fortune and benevolence – would have acted in 1851, given the popular support for Napoleon III. They would, after all, have reached middle age by the time the novel was published, like many of the Second Empire's bourgeois couples. Would they be reading it in exile or in Haussmann's renovated Paris? For all its faith in humanity, *Les Misérables* shared Hugo's inability to do away with doubt.

Unlike Valjean, who dies in his mid-sixties, the sixty-year-old poet and humanitarian was not as close to death as his recent illnesses had caused him to fear. Hugo was living by one of his preferred mottos, *perseverando*,[48] the Spanish present participle from the verb 'to persevere'. Just before *Les Misérables* reached the bookshelves, he started welcoming local impoverished children for lunches at Hauteville House in a tradition known as the 'dîner des pauvres'. He had also condemned the sacking of Beijing's Summer Palace by the British and the French in 1860 during the Second

Opium War.[49] Early in spring 1863, he sent an open letter to the European press, urging Russian soldiers to see their Polish brothers in the January Uprising as an example to be emulated, not an enemy to be massacred. During the siege of Puebla that spring, as the French army tried to establish a monarchy in Mexico, the Second Federal Republic rallied popular support using extracts from *Napoléon le Petit*. 'You have Napoleon, we have Victor Hugo,' the Mexican resisters bragged. 'You are right to think that I am with you,' he responded.[50] Later that year, he answered Giuseppe Garibaldi's request for financial and moral assistance with the Risorgimento. During the remainder of his exile, he publicly supported the Cretan Revolt, Cuba's resistance against Spain, clemency for the Irish Fenians and the abolition of the death penalty in Colombia, Geneva and Portugal.

While completing *Les Misérables*, Hugo had been thinking again about a writer's responsibility to effect change in a series of essays intended to be used as its preface. Caught up in the novel's mammoth growth spurt, these writings soon refocused as an ultimately unfinished preface to his entire oeuvre. They aped the reasoned logic of the eighteenth-century *philosophes* to tease out the limits to man's knowledge in trying to comprehend the universe: 'Science has the first say about everything but the last word about nothing.'[51] He filtered many of these essays' ideas into a publication that he did manage to complete, although one that again outgrew its original function as a preface to his son François-Victor's translations of the complete works of Shakespeare during the bard's tercentenary of 1864.

In truth, *William Shakespeare* was not about Shakespeare. The essay's short opening biography, which would have benefitted from more disciplined research to say the least, gave way to its real subject: the making of artistic genius and, by implication, why Hugo was best suited to fit this bill in the nineteenth century. The misleading title and his argument's self-serving nature predictably drew ridicule from critics. Nonetheless, *William Shakespeare* was as revealing a theorization of Hugo's artistry as the preface to *Cromwell*. Art still needed to engage with both contingent reality and endless possibility, and to use contrasts as a dynamic whole rather than in binary opposition. Politicizing his thinking further, Hugo laid out an extensive line of great minds that had brought civilization to the revolutionary turning points of the late eighteenth century. This dynasty was fraternal and self-governing, not hierarchical or determined by birthright. Each new heir expanded the limits of knowledge, rather than imitated any predecessor, to become one of what Hugo called the *hommes océans*.

From Homer to Shakespeare, these 'ocean men' helped successive generations to come to terms with an endlessly variable but fundamentally free world. They were bound by their innovative spirit in finding ways of expressing 'the infinite, the unknown', and by the hostility they faced from the pedantry of orthodox thinking. They resisted any expectation that art should either be self-sufficient, with no interest in social improvement, or uncritically instrumental in promoting progress, as if human knowledge and behaviour were simply perfectible. Instead, they shone light on the unsettled nature of the human condition, guiding civilization like lighthouses ushering ships across the waves. Their role was to empower society, not to rule or indoctrinate it. 'Being enlightened is entirely the opposite of being subjugated,' thus the struggle against ignorance was a collective rather than individual responsibility in which no one could justify being complicit with oppression. 'Whoever watches a crime happen lets it happen.'[52] These criteria allowed Hugo to lay his claim to literary greatness without having to name himself. The self-absorption of 'art for art's sake' was no more a sign of genius in the nineteenth century than the promises of comprehensive understanding offered by the era's philosophers and scientists.

Publicly, *William Shakespeare* validated Hugo's belief that only the visionary who combined philosophical observation with poetic

Photograph of Victor Hugo by Edmond Bacot, 1862. Hugo here combined his usual contemplative pose with his rebellious streak, turning the chair around and adopting an air of impatience.

intuition could help society move beyond its impasses. Privately, the dutiful poet wanted to clarify to his family why the sacrifices he had made in exile were of such importance. In addition to his wife and eldest son, who were living in Brussels and Paris, his daughter had now left Guernsey under worrying circumstances. The previous summer in 1863, an erratic Adèle had suddenly headed to Halifax to follow a British lieutenant named Albert Pinson. She announced their marriage, but it soon became clear that this was a fabrication and that Pinson had no interest in her. The infatuated Adèle refused to return. She had her father's perseverance and his imagination, but she also had her uncle's poor mental health. Her mother's fears that exile had not been the healthiest of environments for a young single woman were slowly realized. Hugo would not see his daughter again until 1872.

Early in 1865, François-Victor left Guernsey for Brussels and completed the family exodus after the death of his fiancée from tuberculosis. 'I had to choose between my family and my work, between my happiness and my duty,' his father later reflected. 'I chose duty. Such is the law of my life.'[53] Before autumn was over, he published nearly eighty poems that he had been writing since 1859 in *Songs of the Streets and Woods*, which affirmed that poetry could still bring happiness. The title recalled his conflict between public service and withdrawal into nature, and the collection pulled together the lighter, carefree poetry that Hugo had composed as a counterweight to his recent epic endeavours in verse and in fiction. 'Be pure in spirit; simply act./ Nothing is low when souls are high.'[54] Gone were the colossal columns of august alexandrines and daring ventures, replaced by shorter stanzas and swifter metres in a reminder that his contemplative stance had not robbed him of his poetic agility.

Struggle and endurance continued to occupy Hugo's thoughts, however. It was no coincidence that he held the Book of Job in the highest esteem, or that Job's ordeals qualified him as one of the 'ocean men'. *The Toilers of the Sea*, which was a best-seller in the spring of 1866, was a philosophical follow-up to both *Notre-Dame de Paris* and *Les Misérables*. Where those novels consider fate through the lenses of religious belief and social prejudice respectively, *The Toilers of the Sea* looks at humankind's relationship with the natural elements and rounds out what the novel's preface calls a 'triple *ananke*' (recalling the keyword of fate or necessity from *Notre-Dame de Paris*). In a sign that any support received during exile was of immense value to him, Hugo dedicated the novel to 'the island of Guernsey, hard and kind, my present asylum, my probable tomb'. In addition to the island's welcome, he had felt fortified by its surroundings on his walks down the southeastern coastal path to Fermain Bay or up the west coast to the Grandes Rocques, whose sepia-toned, rough-textured formations were mirrored in the visuals of the browned pen-and-ink washes that he created for a planned illustrated edition.

In the novel, inventive engineering and dedicated grind, as the drivers of nineteenth-century industry, combine with the resilience and heroism of the labours of Hercules. The resourceful Gilliatt is a gruff fisherman who shuns social interaction but who harbours a love for the beautiful Déruchette. When her uncle's prize steamboat the *Durande* runs aground on the perilous Roches-Douvres reef, Déruchette offers to marry whoever can salvage the vessel's engine. Physically versatile and forever attentive to his surroundings, Gilliatt embarks upon a scintillating two-month clash against nature. Armed only with a saw, hatchet, chisel and hammer, he single-handedly clears the wreck of debris, learns to live on and off the rocks, battles a fierce equinoxal storm and defeats a hungry giant octopus – *la pieuvre* – which had claimed the life of the ship's captain. The prolonged focus on these toils allowed Hugo to philosophize about nature's incalculable powers of creation and destruction without digressing as patently as he had done in *Les Misérables*. In his solitude, Gilliatt feels 'the unknown that is within us fraternizing

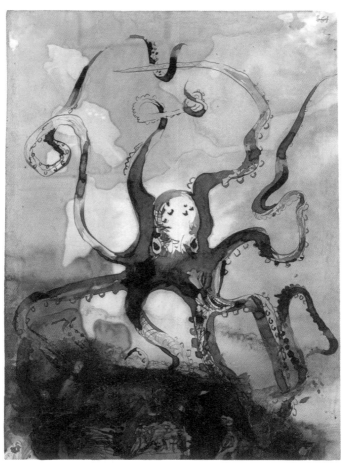

Victor Hugo, *La Pieuvre*, *c*. 1866, pen and brown ink wash. One of Hugo's 36 illustrations for *The Toilers of the Sea* – the only one of his novels that he chose to illustrate. The octopus's suckered tentacles curl into the initials vh at the top, leaving Hugo's mark on an image that, like so many of his drawings, combines grace with dread.

mysteriously with an unknown that is outside of us . . . What anguish, and at the same time what delight!'[55]

Unfortunately for Gilliatt, Hugo was not about to let this gladiator unite with the object of his desire. Gilliatt returns triumphant from the reef but overhears Déruchette's confession of love to another man, Ebenezer, along with her disgust at the thought of having to marry her uncle's socially awkward and unkempt saviour. Like Quasimodo's attempts to unite Esmeralda and Phoebus or Valjean rescuing Marius for Cosette, Gilliatt arranges for the couple to be together, only then to surrender to death (in this case, letting himself be swallowed by the rising tide while watching their ship sail away). The outcome of Gilliatt's astonishing efforts on his reef articulated Hugo's recurring anxieties about his own trials on 'my old rock': that personal sacrifice, though critical to others' needs, could result in rejection and unbearable loss.

Hugo may not have been willing to let his novel end on the high notes of stage comedy, but he had returned to writing for the theatre nevertheless. His stagecraft had not completely slipped from view during exile thanks to Gaetano Donizetti's opera of *Lucrezia Borgia* and Verdi's *Rigoletto* (based on *The King Takes his Amusement*). The imperial ban of his theatre was lifted in 1867, making way for a Paris revival of *Hernani*. Hugo had been commissioned to write the introduction to the *Paris Guide* for the International Exposition that began two months before the play reappeared. With France welcoming the world to its capital throughout the spring and summer, it could not afford to shelve its most renowned writer. Hugo, for his part, did not trust the Empire's motives, and sure enough the ban was restored before the year was out due to his ongoing support for Garibaldi.

Freed from any expectation that he would stage what he wrote, he penned ten sometimes incomplete pieces during and immediately after exile, which were published posthumously as *Theatre in Freedom*. All but one of these were written in the late 1860s. His moral conscience was strong in *The Intervention*'s tragi-comedy of a grieving couple bound by poverty but tempted by infidelity, and in the religious fanaticism of *Torquemada*'s Spanish Inquisition, while his playfulness was clear in the Shakespearean fairy tale *The Sodden Forest* and in the baroque verse comedy *Will They Eat?* Their diverse forms showcased a playwright transitioning from nineteenth-century Romantic drama to the innovative theatre of the twentieth century.

By the time his next novel, *The Man Who Laughs*, was published in the spring of 1869, Hugo had even less reason to imagine a comedic ending than he had for *The Toilers of the Sea*. Charles and his wife Alice, whom he had married in 1865, had lost their first-born son, Georges, to meningitis. A second son, also called Georges, was born in August 1868, but eleven days later Hugo's wife died in Brussels following a heart attack. Adèle senior had continued to support his career since starting to spend more time away, acting as his representative in Paris when *Les Misérables* appeared and publishing her deferential biography of him in 1863 (edited by Vacquerie and Meurice). She had even struck up diplomatic relations with Juliette. It was obvious nonetheless that Hugo's first love had been leading a more independent life. Death completed that separation. 'I am overwhelmed with grief but hopeful,' he noted. 'I await the supreme life in death.'[56] He did not do so alone: five days after Adèle's death, his diary alluded to payment to a certain Louise in Brussels.

The Man Who Laughs is best known as the basis for a 1928 silent film that inspired the look of the Batman villain, the Joker, who debuted in the Detective Comics series in 1940. The novel's disfigured hero, Gwynplaine, has more in common with the Caped Crusader as an orphan seeking justice rather than spreading chaos, even if the malevolent Joker offers an intriguing slant on Hugo's questions of individual accountability. Gwynplaine had been mutilated by child traffickers who carved a perpetual grin

Photograph of Juliette Drouet in Brussels by Arsène Garnier, *c.* 1868.

into his face. In young adulthood, he tours the carnivals of southern Britain at the turn of the eighteenth century with his surrogate father, Ursus, and the blind Dea. Following several coincidences and revelations, he discovers that he is the son of a rebel lord and that the despotic King James II was responsible for his disfigurement. He attacks the country's inequality in the House of Lords but his appearance provokes only laughter. He renounces his new aristocratic status to reunite with Dea, but events have proved overwhelming and she dies in his arms. Overcome, Gwynplaine throws himself into the Thames.

Another novel, another suicidal ending that points to death as the only resolution possible for a character's social and emotional quandaries. One way in which *The Man Who Laughs* distinguishes itself, however, is by dramatizing more overtly than before the tensions that Hugo's lust provoked. An opposition between love and sex is presented through Gwynplaine's desires for both the wholesome Dea and the wanton Duchess Josiana, who lures him into her private chambers where he feels himself 'start to combust in a heavenly swelter'.[57] Conspicuously for nineteenth-century French fiction and for a writer for whom supposedly nothing was off limits, Hugo's heroes are all chaste. They suggest a de-sexed ideal that held persistent sway over his imagination, but such purity came under pressure. In particular, Gilliatt's battle with the *pieuvre* staged a contest between a shirtless, powerful hero and a creature likened to the Gorgon Medusa. Described as being all suckers and kisses, the octopus is an embodied erotic nightmare, embracing Gilliatt tightly with its octet of phallic tentacles as he tries to save himself from being swallowed into the cephalopod's mouth. Sexual contact is equated with a violent loss of self, as it is in Frollo's explosions of rage towards Esmeralda in *Notre-Dame de Paris*. When Gwynplaine wrestles with his feelings, the stakes of such encounters are made starker and simpler: listen to his heart or his body. Disconnected from his family and torn between the saintly Dea and the sexualized Josiana, his creator's own fears and impulses are never far away.

The plot contains all the expected elements of Hugo's fiction, including displaced families, whimsical characters and tested virtue, but *The Man Who Laughs* was a commercial disappointment. Readers were impatient with the digressions on topics such as architecture and genealogy, which seemed particularly demanding and heavy-handed, and which matched the hero's risk of sexual excess with the author's information overload. They also found little in the book's critiques of late Restoration Britain that related to the challenges of the nineteenth century, such as industrialization and rising nationalism. Furthermore, the book's timing was questionable, as France's attention was fixed on parliamentary elections later that spring.

Those elections offered Hugo something to refocus on. Napoleon iii looked vulnerable in the wake of scandals, strikes and growing opposition. Weeks before the first round of voting, Hugo's sons took advantage of relaxed newspaper laws on ministerial consent to found *Le Rappel* ('The Reminder'). The regime won a majority but could not win over urban workers, who helped the mainly republican opposition secure major gains. The emperor's foreign affairs did not bode well either, due to the threat posed by the North German Confederation that Prussian Chancellor Otto von Bismarck had established after military victories against Denmark and Austria. Hugo chaired a Peace Congress in Lausanne for the League of Peace and Freedom, which had been founded in 1867 with the support of Louis Blanc, John Bright, Garibaldi, Herzen and John Stuart Mill, among others. He stressed that war benefitted only leaders and never the people. But a successful plebiscite on the Empire's policies in May 1870 gave Napoleon iii renewed confidence. Two months later, Bismarck edited the Ems Telegram to goad France into military aggression and to bring the southern German regions to his side.

Hugo planted an acorn in Hauteville House's lawn to sow hope. He predicted that the oak tree would rise like the United States of Europe, which would crown the old world while its sister republic in North America led the new one. In the meantime, it was inevitable that the two countries he had seen as the axis of that republic would take up arms. On 19 July, France declared war. Hugo and Juliette soon travelled with Charles and his family to Brussels. It had fast become clear that the French army was not as dominant as the Empire's propaganda had believed, so he and his sons were prepared to fight for the National Guard if needed. The news of the emperor's surrender at the Battle of Sedan on 2 September was bittersweet. Hugo's perseverance had finally been rewarded and the Empire was collapsing, but France was under invasion. On 5 September, he took a train back into the country that he had not stepped foot within for almost twenty years.

5

'I am a man of revolution' (1870–85)

In the spring of 1871, as France threatened to break apart in the aftermath of the Franco-Prussian War, Hugo held on to his belief that the French Revolution had shaped who he was. 'During my adolescence I was that man of revolution without even knowing it. My education was keeping me in the past while my instincts pushed me towards the future. I was a political royalist but a literary revolutionary.' As the soon-to-be septuagenarian pondered the future, he remained focused on the need for thinking to be open-minded and for behaviour to be non-partisan. 'Conciliation in our ideas and reconciliation in our actions' had to be prioritized to make a fairer and more harmonious world.[1]

This conciliatory and pacifist spirit was not to be mistaken for some genteel and imperturbable manner, however. Hugo had no intention of comfortably settling into old age. His image from his final fifteen years is that of the white-bearded republican survivor, whose patriarchal stature was immortalized in photographs by Étienne Carjat, Nadar and others, but the ageing grandfather was still young at heart. Achille Mélandri's 1881 photograph showed Hugo seated on a couch with his grandson Georges on one side and his granddaughter Jeanne (who had been born the year after her brother) on the other. Hugo had lowered his head to the same height as his diminutive grand-children and was drawing them tightly towards him in a jovial embrace. This was not an authoritative elder waving his finger

Achille Mélandri, *The Art of Being a Grandfather*, 1881. Photograph of Victor Hugo with Jeanne (left) and Georges (right).

with moral self-certainty, but an old man beaming with glee at being part of this young playgroup.

Mélandri's image, which bore the same title as Hugo's 1877 poetry collection *The Art of Being a Grandfather*, offered visual confirmation of what the poet continued to express in words. Hugo understood that insight was derived not from the affectations of old age, but from creation's enterprising spirit. He refused to be hemmed in by the clichés of seniority. At the end of that volume's sixth book, appropriately entitled 'Grand Old Age and Kneehigh Mixed', he described himself as 'unsure of being sure, prone even to some doubt'. 'Do not raise me up to the rank of the good Lord!', he demanded. If he was to be modelled on God in the French imagination, he wanted it to be the truly divine, through which the received wisdom of axioms and judgemental authority was to be rebelliously questioned, not calmly accepted and peddled.[2]

Maintaining this iconoclastic thrust helped him to preserve his vitality. The knowledge that the end was nearing energized him to make use of what time he had left, as it had done in exile. The grand old man of the French Republic was afforded no illusions about the inescapability of his body's eventual collapse: during the 1870s the last of his Romantic Cénacle would die (Dumas in December 1870 and Gautier in October 1872), and all three of his remaining children would succumb to different tragedies. As death approached, life still beckoned. When confronting the calamitous events of the Franco-Prussian War and the Paris Commune, he was finally able to grasp the nettle that he had stepped around in previous work, namely the French Revolution's violent descent into the Terror of 1793. Whether as a writer or as a re-elected public official, the grandfatherly Hugo believed he had nothing to lose by telling the fledgling Third Republic what he thought it needed to hear if it was to prosper. His prolific outputs in exile ensured that, even after a stroke in 1878, the editing and publication of pre-existing material would keep his visionary voice alive.

This zest for life also sustained his physical desires. His continuing exercises in virility showed both the reckless abandon and obsessive compulsion of a man increasingly aware of his own mortality. His love of women did not wane, nor did his conflict between amorous sentiment and sexual pleasure. One of the poems from the second cycle of *The Legend of the Ages* in 1877, 'Homo Duplex' ('Man is Twofold'), curtly summarized this friction between his emotions and his anatomy. A duke is hunting in the forest (one of Hugo's erotic metaphors in his diary) and happens upon an angel and an ape who are in combat with one another as representatives of his soul and body. The duke is told that each of his virtuous deeds enlarges his soul's wingspan while each sin empowers the beast. When he dies, he will either see daybreak or darkness deepen, 'for I [the angel] will lift you up or he [the ape] will eat you whole'.[3] The contest between collective moral duty and unchecked individual desire that Hugo feared in France's post-Revolutionary history was one that played out at a more intimate level for him. Caught between compunction and compulsion, his life and work still bore the weight of the Revolution, not only of its ideals but also its excesses.

1870–73: From Hero to Heretic

Shortly after his train crossed the border on the afternoon of 5 September, Hugo saw an encampment of French soldiers. He called out 'Vive l'armée!' and cried. That evening, an enthusiastic crowd awaited his arrival in Paris's Gare du Nord. He noted hearing 'Vive Victor Hugo' and verses being recited from *Châtiments*. 'In one hour you have rewarded me for nineteen years of exile,' he told them.[4] The festivities lasted well into the night, but an emotional Hugo had not come back to rejoice. The Prussian army was marching unopposed towards the city. Fast-acting deputies from the National Assembly had established the Government of National Defence, and Hugo saw himself as one of the many national resources to be mobilized.

On 9 September, the French press published his appeal to the Germans. He repeated his thinking from the *Paris Guide* of 1867 by lauding Paris as a shared symbol of civilization. 'Paris is yours as much as ours . . . There was Athens, there was Rome, and now there's Paris.' He asked what sense this war had now that their mutual enemy, Napoleon III, had been defeated, and he warned that any attack would bring shame on the German people.[5] The message was not well received across the Rhine, so he criticized the European powers for not intervening and then called his compatriots to arms. 'If the lights of Paris go out, Europe will be plunged into darkness.'[6] On 19 September, the city had been surrounded and the siege of Paris began.

Devoted to the City of Light, Hugo had chosen not to leave beforehand, unlike a number of others who could afford to relocate. He donated the first profits from Hetzel's new edition of *Châtiments* to the war effort and waived copyright permissions for public readings of those poems so that the proceeds could fund cannons on the city's ramparts. The siege demanded unselfishness. Two attempts to break the blockade failed, and fuel and food shortages were made worse by a harsh winter. Parisians resorted to eating horses, then dogs, cats, rats and even the zoo animals at the Jardin des Plantes. It was a steep fall from grace for a city that three years earlier had welcomed the world to the Universal Exposition. These privations strengthened Hugo's will. 'I am hungry and cold. So much the better. I suffer what the people suffer.'[7] His contact with various officials and activists who consulted him for advice firmed up this connection, as did the availability of the city's actresses and courtesans.

The war had made a federation of European republics look impossible, but its fallout was yet more damaging to his hopes for the future. Paris held out for over four months until the government finally surrendered on 28 January. National elections were held less than a fortnight later, as per the armistice agreement, to prepare for peace negotiations. Hugo was returned as a Parisian deputy and headed to Bordeaux, where the National Assembly temporarily convened. France was deeply divided rather than united. The rural vote gave two-thirds of seats to conservative factions, but the urban electorate and especially Paris chose republican candidates. The right-wing majority favoured a constitutional monarchy but their disagreement over which of the two bloodlines (the Bourbons or Orléans) should rule was further complicated by challenges from the Bonapartists. The republicans faced their own splits between the moderates, the radicals and the far left. The former Orléanist prime minister and opponent of Napoleon III, the 73-year-old Adolphe Thiers, became chief executive, believing that republicanism 'is the system of government that divides us the least'.[8] His pragmatism served him well when he had to be the bearer of bad news and announce Bismarck's final terms: massive indemnity payments and war reparations, as well as the loss of the major industrial region of Alsace and part of Lorraine on the border.

Hugo's first parliamentary address on 1 March foresaw what Thiers knew. This humiliation would condemn Europe to future war by emboldening the Germans' imperial ambitions and by leaving the French vengeful. Better to renew the conflict now, Hugo argued, but more cautious heads prevailed and the armistice was approved. After the Assembly voted to relocate to Versailles the following week and opposed Garibaldi's election in Algeria, Hugo resigned. His hopelessly idealistic, if not suicidal, support for the war effort and his decision to stand down betrayed his disbelief at what was happening. France was to be crippled, and the cost of care would be footed by tax hikes and debt interests that would hit the poorest the hardest. Worse still, the Assembly's choice of Versailles over Paris in the wake of demonstrations that had occurred in the besieged capital showed that the political class was still afraid of the country's revolutionary past. The bitter memories of June 1848, the Empire's shortcomings in social policy and the creation of the International Workingmen's Association in 1864 had made the city's working-class boroughs in the north and east ache for radical change.

The patriarch mourning his country became the father grieving for his son when Charles unexpectedly died from a brain haemorrhage. Homeland and household were equally painful for Hugo when the family buried Charles in Paris on 18 March. That same day, when army soldiers tried to take control of Paris's cannons to disarm the unsettled city, disgruntled residents and National Guardsmen fought back. Two captured generals were violently killed. The Central Committee of the National Guard assumed command of the city under the socialist red flag and called local elections to establish an independent municipal authority. Fortunately for Hugo, he had to leave Paris with his family shortly after Charles's funeral to deal with his son's estate in Brussels. He felt that the *Versaillais* government and the Parisian *fédérés* had each wanted to fulfil France's historical role as a national republic and a beacon of equality respectively, but that both sides had acted precipitously. 'In wanting to snuff out political discord,' he claimed, 'Thiers has ignited social war.'[9] With similar impartiality, he believed that 'the Commune is a good thing badly done'.[10]

Hugo published poems that warned against escalating the aggression, since France would be 'murdering its soul' in an act of shocking self-harm. The government's bombardments and the Commune's fervour had put both the Arc de Triomphe and Vendôme Column at risk, and the Communards threatened reprisals against hostages for the army's execution of prisoners. 'Be just: that is how we best serve the republic.'[11] Now it was the turn of the French not to heed his pleas. When the army advanced on the city's western fortifications on 21 May to retake the city, France's 'Bloody Week' ensued. Historians continue to debate the number of those killed in the vicious street fighting or summarily executed, but even revised estimates of the well-worn figure of 20,000 put the death toll between 7,000 and 10,000.[12] Before their last stand, the Communards set alight many of the city's centres of power such as the Tuileries Palace and the Hôtel de Ville, in addition to killing the archbishop of Paris and other hostages.

As France's heart bled and burned, the *Belgian Independence* published Hugo's letter protesting Belgium's decision to deport any fleeing Communards to face trial. He condemned a horrendous moral failing on both sides but, controversially, he offered asylum in his Brussels residence on the basis that 'ignorance is not the fault of the ignorant'.[13] An angry mob made their displeasure felt outside the house and the Belgian government expelled Hugo from the country. Rather than return to France to witness the government's reprisals as it sentenced, deported or executed thousands of prisoners, he moved to Luxembourg, where he remained until going back to Paris in late September. As had been the case in the early 1850s, exile reinvigorated his determination to help piece back together the wreckage of a republic that had run aground.

He started by asking France to confront the horrors of what had happened in a collection of 98 poems entitled *The Terrible Year*. Hugo looked upon these twelve months with his eye for both uncomfortable detail and moral significance. Written almost entirely in alexandrines and rhyming couplets, it had none of the variety that propelled *Châtiments*, but its implacably solemn pace and grave tone captured his severity of feeling. His disgust with human conflict ('Grisly blood-drinker, withered reprobate/ Luring mankind into his drunken state') and his insistence on forgiveness ('My crime in this land was to offer help') power *The Terrible Year*'s conscience.[14]

Hugo's capacity for anger and compassion brought him to condemn his old enemies of the unenlightened human mind and insufficient social welfare in an implicit assault on the upper and middle classes. In 'With Whom Lies the Fault?', he harangues an arsonist who has set a library ablaze ('It's your own torch that you have just blown out!'), but the poet's tirade is ended by the firebug's meek response ('I don't know how to read'). The weight of indignation is offset by a simple reminder of civilization's incompletion. This realization is more upsetting in 'The Shot', in which the poet believes a dead child should stir more pity than the sight of the Tuileries ablaze.[15] He also ensures that the reader does not mistake the spiritual force that guides his moral compass. If the reader has in mind 'some fellow with a long white beard,/ as in a pope or emperor', then the poet happily declares himself an atheist. The final poem also warns that the true divine exceeds all mortal control. An anxious old world calls out to God to persuade history's tide to recede, but it is this same fluid mass that emotionlessly responds: 'You thought me the tide and I am the flood.'[16] The unstoppable floodwaters offer an ambivalent image of both fate's indifference and natural transformation.

Before the first edition of *The Terrible Year* was published and sold out, Hugo failed to get re-elected to the Assembly at the start of 1872, although he still secured 45 per cent of the available vote against the government's candidate. A far greater loss would occupy his thoughts when his youngest daughter finally returned to France in February accompanied by a freed slave, Céline Alvarez Baa, who had been looking after her. Adèle had been in Barbados, still following Pinson. Now mentally withdrawn and talking mostly to herself, upon her return she was quietly moved to a comfortable asylum just outside of Paris. Visits were to be kept to a minimum. Her father's hopes that Adèle's return to his side would bring her to her senses and back to good health were dashed. She would spend the remaining 43 years of her life at the institution.

That summer he moved back to Guernsey with what was left of his family after the unremitting storm of the past two years. He wanted to finish a novel that he had first envisaged nearly a decade earlier. The subject – the war in the Vendée between the Republic and the *ancien régime* during the Reign of Terror in 1793 – had taken on renewed urgency. Only the vantage points of his lookout across the sea could help him free up the necessary depth of vision with which to peer into such a darkened moment in French history. Paris had too many distractions, especially as he had enjoyed the intimate company of numerous women since returning, including Gautier's daughter Judith and the famous actress Sarah Bernhardt (both in their late twenties), as well as Adèle's companion Madame Baa ('The first Negress in my life').

Although his diary noted suggestively three occasions when he and Juliette were together in the winter 'as we were 40 years ago', physical congress between them had been rare.[17] He still preferred to elevate their relationship to an unequalled and asexual level. 'Love is more than a union: it is unity . . . Lovers are linked by their souls.'[18] In contrast, his libido was easily tempted by less transcendental experiences. Whether it was the purity of love or the passion of lust, he found himself irresistibly drawn by his feelings, but at the same time markedly unsure about their sustainability and about his freedom to follow them. A woman's allure had ample potential to become oppressive:

> When their affections have been gained,
> > Then we begin our slavery.
> Friend, would you learn their ABC?
> It spells adored, bekissed, and chained.[19]

A new domination loomed. Juliette's new maid, Blanche Lanvin, aroused Hugo in ways he had not felt since his relationship with Léonie. The small brunette in her early twenties was responsible for cryptic concerns in his diary that reflected his awareness of a dangerous desire for her, which was consummated in the spring of 1873. Juliette soon suspected the attraction and dismissed her back to France. Blanche secretly returned, only for the lovers to be spotted and for her to be sent back to Paris once again. With his novel close to completion and François-Victor unwell, Hugo had additional incentive to return to the capital at the end of July.

Juliette's suspicions were soon confirmed and in September she furiously left the city for a week. Hugo spent several panicked days wondering where she had gone and if she would ever return. Once she came back (from Brussels), they reunited and he promised not to continue his liaison. Unsurprisingly, it was a promise he did not manage to keep. For the man who had noted to himself that he was no 'dealer of used books' when it came to his tastes in women, what had been true earlier in his life remained ever the case.[20] The rush of sexual pleasure and the ardour of youth had too exhilarating an effect on his body and his mind to be resisted, but he was still conscious of how such liberation also entailed a loss of self-possession. A line he had written in July that 'devourers are themselves devoured – strange fate!' when thinking about the self-interest of tyrants revealed a more general apprehension about individual will.[21]

Juliette had long played an impossible role in his life. She was integral to the worth he wanted to see in himself as a poet and a partner. But she was also essential to the value of his transgressions with other women as an opportunity to feel both the elation and emptiness of self-release. His excesses relied on having a point of continuity to digress from and turn back towards. The woman who knew him best diagnosed a trauma, in a language that borrowed from his mix of the metaphorical with the unadulterated:

You are suffering from an open wound – that of women – that keeps getting larger, because you do not have the courage to cauterize it once and for all. As for me, I suffer from loving you too much. We have, each of us, our incurable ills.[22]

The latter statement was unfortunately true for François-Victor as well. Hugo's youngest son died during the Christmas period from tuberculosis, the disease of artists and the urban poor. In a touching tribute to his deceased sons, he pondered how 'the clock that has struck for the sons will perhaps one day soon strike for the father'.[23]

1874–7: Being a Patriarch

Any fear that Hugo would become paralysed with grief was allayed by the publication of *Ninety-Three* in February 1874. He used his pen to scratch away rebelliously at the national wounds that *The Terrible Year* had opened so as to continue treating the sickness that had plagued France since 1789, namely the inability to come to terms with the Revolution and to make its fraternal ideal a reality. The bitter clash between the Commune and the government in 1871 recalled the vicious civil war of 1793 in the Vendée between the populist uprising that had started in Paris in 1789 and the royalist forces seeking to re-establish power from the provinces. In *Ninety-Three*'s efforts to find common ground between a rebellious Vendée loyal to the crown and the committed believers in the Revolution's meritocracy, the novel excavated not just national history for Hugo: the memory of his parents' divergent world views and his fractious family origins also pervaded its writing.

To make the historical connection between the Terror and 1871, *Ninety-Three* is Hugo's most violent novel. The characters and the regional setting are infused with blinding savagery. The Channel's furious waters, the monstrous woodlands that swallow men whole and the ravenous fire of the climax all reveal an untamed nature in keeping with the plot's graphic bloodletting and wanton destruction. The summary executions, mass graves and burning properties in the month of May 1793 would of course have brought back memories of the Commune's 'Bloody Week'. He used the continuity of these schisms between revolutionary idealism and reactionary conservatism to emphasize that neither had definitively suppressed the other in nearly a century. If the dream of 1789 of a fair and equitable France was to be realized, then a less hostile and more cooperative relationship would be needed between these competing visions.

Purposely written in words rather than numbers, the novel's title implied that only the allegorical possibilities of literature could bring the nation to this understanding of itself, as opposed to a simply factual or unsentimental approach. 'I have tried,' Hugo noted, 'to introduce into what we call politics the question of morality and humanity.'[24] *Ninety-Three* depicts the Royalist insurrection of the Chouannerie in Brittany, which looks to the Marquis de Lantenac to lead the revolt. The National Convention dispatches the cold Cimourdain to suppress the uprising, whose republicanism owes as much to Draco as to Plato (and who made an impression on a teenage Joseph Stalin). Linking the two ruthless foes is the commander of the region's republican forces, Gauvain, who was Cimourdain's student, but who is also, in one of Hugo's bolder coincidences, Lantenac's great nephew. Cimourdain used to be a priest and Gauvain comes from the nobility yet they both fight for the Revolution, while Lantenac's aristocratic background is at odds with the guerrilla fighting he coordinates.

This characterization primes Hugo's familiar reversals of fortune. His sensitivity towards how dividing lines can quickly shift brings dramatic intensity to the novel's interests in fraternity and forgiveness. To these ends, Gauvain's name promises heroism, borrowed as it is from King Arthur's nephew and one of the Round Table's most compassionate knights. The triangular relationship carries *Ninety-Three* towards a climactic battle at the chateau where Gauvain grew up, called La Tourgue and knowingly described as the 'Breton Bastille'. Here Lantenac's dwindled regiment fends off the much larger revolutionary forces. Gauvain's great uncle ultimately sacrifices his chance at escape to save three refugee children who are trapped inside the blazing building. Gauvain responds in kind by symbolically allowing Lantenac to escape wearing his own republican uniform. Like him, Gauvain accepts that such self-sacrifice will be fatal.

In the final scene, the single-minded Cimourdain signs Gauvain's execution order but shoots himself as the guillotine's blade descends on the young commandant. The ending evokes a natural order of reciprocity: compassion begets pity, but to administer death is to damn yourself. The narrator pointedly asks what kind of republic can therefore triumph: 'the republic of terror or the republic of clemency? Victory through severity or through compassion?'[25] The question of whether this challenge for the future would be accepted was far from resolved, but *Ninety-Three* enjoyed strong sales and was translated into ten languages.

Its success gave Hugo further confidence in making the case for full amnesty towards the Communards. In 1875 he began publishing his collected speeches and public interventions since the 1840s in *Deeds and Words*. These volumes integrated the republican who had chosen exile with the poet who had repeatedly pleaded for leniency towards outcasts. Hugo also lined up a pre-emptive strike on those who continued to accuse him of poetic silliness: 'Foresight, when it's projected too far into the future, raises only a smile. To tell an egg that it has wings seems absurd, yet it is the truth.'[26] He continued this conversation in person. With Juliette's support, he regularly welcomed guests to a salon at his new home in Paris's ninth arrondissement, where they lived with his daughter-in-law Alice and his grandchildren. The apartments were on the Rue de Clichy, which ran from the working hub of Montmartre (home to some of the Commune's strongest support) to the stylish bourgeois haunts clustered around the Opéra. Over the years, visitors included republicans like Jules Simon, Léon Gambetta, Louis Blanc and the future 'Tiger' of the Great War, Georges Clemenceau, in addition to literary admirers such as Charles Swinburne and Ivan Turgenev, as well as international dignitaries such as Pedro II of Brazil.

In January 1876, Hugo was elected to the Senate, which had been reinstated under the new Constitution of the previous year as the upper chamber of the French Parliament. He had no expectation of himself as anything other than an authentic voice in a political forum that could be both factional and belligerent. He did not write the kind of memorable Assembly speeches recorded in *Deeds and Words* as he was now fully reinvested in communicating directly with the public. In late August, he published an article in *Le Rappel* demanding that the European powers support those Balkan principalities that had fought back against the Ottoman Empire's rule. His desire to 'replace political questions with human ones' pinpointed why he was not suited to the machinations and manoeuvrings of politics: he preferred to speak his mind rather than charm or coerce his fellow politicians. 'What is happening in Serbia demonstrates the necessity of the United States of Europe,' he wrote. 'Let united peoples succeed disunited governments. Let us be done with murderous empires, let us muzzle fanaticism and despotism.' Instead of identifying as one of the political class, the new senator actively distinguished his politics of conscience from what he saw as the 'myopia' of statecraft.[27]

A new cycle of *The Legend of the Ages* in February 1877 reiterated his cosmic visions of history as unrestrained creation, which continued to be opposed by the systematic world of kings. Those visions' insistence on the universe's free nature was repeated three months later in *The Art of Being a Grandfather*. Nearly seventy new poems celebrated the curiosity and playfulness of his beloved grandchildren, who reconnected him with his imagination. He doted on Georges and Jeanne much as he had done with his own children. He had been their legal guardian until their mother's remarriage in April, before the book was published, to a republican politician called Édouard Lockroy. 'He acted our age, spoke our language, liked what we liked,' Georges said of his 'Papapa', remembering their games of hide-and-seek and how Hugo transformed the living room into a wilderness where he pretended to be a lion.[28]

Childlike innocence had long fascinated Hugo as a counterforce to the smothering rationality of adulthood. The street urchin Gavroche is the most memorable example, rebelling against authority and choosing heart over greed, but *Ninety-Three* had also introduced three characters drawn from the same sketch – the three Fléchard children who have been taken by Lantenac's men and who, to entertain themselves, gleefully rip apart an antique gospel they find in La Tourgue's library. History's neatly ordered narratives are always at risk around children in Hugo's literature, hence the poet himself vows in the first of the book's eighteen parts to tear up charters and bibles.[29]

The Art of Being a Grandfather lay in recognizing how much there was to be learned from a child's world of adventure and make-believe. By the same token, Hugo painted himself as a permissive rather than punitive patriarch who was interested not in asserting his individual authority over future generations but in encouraging their creative will. Like *Songs of the Streets and Woods*, his carefree approach to versification marked a conscious departure from his hulking epics in his determination to position himself on the side of youth, not least in a France whose younger poets were following Baudelaire's example and experimenting ever more audaciously with suggestion, irregularity and cadence. The mighty elder of modern France is humbled by two small children who help him wriggle free from restriction. 'I believe in children as I might apostles', since their undeveloped and unsocialized minds grant access to a natural vigour.[30]

The poem 'On Dry Bread' represented one of the more barefaced examples of his appreciation. Jeanne is rationed to bread due to naughtiness. Moved by 'the little exile', her grandfather sneaks her a pot of jam. She promises not to touch her nose with her toes again, or to agitate her grandfather's cat (an indolent but strong-minded soul called Gavroche). Caught in the act, however, a shamed poet is chided by his family for breaking the rules. 'She sees you laughing when we get angry,' they complain, noting that he too deserves to be rationed. Jeanne softly adds that she will bring him some jam if that happens. Whereas the family objectify 'the child', the poet uses Jeanne's proper name, indicating a greater attention to her as a person-in-the-making. The almost oxymoronic penultimate lines, in which her eyes are 'filled with the authority of kindly creatures', rethinks the notion of dominion as the rewarding ability to sympathize with the disobedient rather than simply penalize them.[31] A charitable, even humble attitude was, for Hugo, more likely to attain the desired virtues.

Events at the National Assembly proved once again that this kind of tolerance did not impede him from taking a moral stand. The popular Patrice de MacMahon, who had led the army's suppression of the Commune, had succeeded Thiers as president of the Republic four years earlier thanks in part to the Duc de Broglie's monarchist opposition. The elections of 1876 had given republican deputies the advantage in the Chamber, confirming Thiers' adage that the Republic was the least divisive system of government, but in May 1877 MacMahon dismissed the republican prime minister, Jules Simon, and appointed Broglie. He then dissolved Parliament after a vote of no confidence in the new government. With the Church's full backing and through various acts of censorship, MacMahon looked determined to establish a new constitutional monarchy.

Hugo's main contribution to the republican campaign was a well-timed reminder of what had happened in 1851. *History of a Crime*, which he had started in 1852 but left to one side for *Napoleon le Petit* and *Châtiments*, was a biography of Louis-Napoleon's *coup d'état*. This criminal act is characterized as a fall backwards and one that undid the democratic work that France had carried out:

'Everything that had been built up in the edifice was now in ruins.'[32] Bringing a dramatist's eye to history, Hugo again found himself discovering parallels between France's present and past. The stirring of popular opinion in the name of social order and the collusion of the clergy felt uncannily familiar. The first volume of *History of a Crime* was published in early October and sold over 20,000 copies, just weeks after Hugo had taken part in Thiers' funeral, which had become a mass demonstration of republican opposition to MacMahon. At the end of the month, after both rounds of voting in the elections, republican deputies had only lost a modest percentage of their majority. MacMahon's gamble had not paid off. By the senatorial elections in January 1879, the monarchists would lose control of the upper chamber, leading to MacMahon's resignation and the first truly republican president with no royalist past, Jules Grévy. Hugo believed that the age of republicanism and political cooperation had finally arrived.

1878–85: A Beckoning Light

He was not done with those he saw to be the Republic's enemies in the monarchist-clerical right. In *The Pope* in April 1878, it was the Catholic Church's turn. Written several years earlier, this long philosophical poem envisaged what kind of spiritual leadership the papacy might embody were it to expand its outlook. Asleep, an unnamed pontiff wanders in his dreams into encounters with powerbrokers like royalty and the priesthood, and into the social realities of poverty and war. Over a series of dialogues and soliloquies, he questions his mission as 'the Patriarch of the West'. Leaving Rome for Jerusalem in a symbolic pilgrimage towards Christ, he calls for an end to conflict and to human ills: 'Free beneath the blue sky,/ equals in the face of death, all brothers / before the Father . . . Peace and forgiveness.' But the poem ends with one of Hugo's favourite devices: an isolated final expression that abruptly turns the line of thought in a different direction to jolt the reader out of complacency. The pope wakes up and exclaims, 'What a dreadful dream I have had!'[33] His unconscious mind was open to God's calling, but his pontifical reason dismisses these insights. Hugo's satirical derogation of the papacy discredited the Vicars of Christ that he had seen come and go. The new pope, Leo XIII, maintained the Vatican's opposition to the Italian government, and his predecessor, Pius IX, was guilty in Hugo's eyes of dogmatically defining papal infallibility, in addition to enabling the Second Empire's crookery.

By no coincidence, Hugo addressed the celebrations in May for the centenary of Voltaire's death as the French Enlightenment's most satirical defender of free religion and free speech. For all the honours and invitations that Hugo received, he responded by lauding the writer's public responsibility. 'Voltaire declared war on the coalition of social iniquities and accepted the fight. And what was his weapon? One as light as the wind and with the force of lightning: a pen.' In June, he delivered the opening address at the International Literary Congress during the third Paris World's Fair, which had opened as a showcase for France's recovery. He spoke of the need to build a public literary domain in which 'the book, as a book, belongs to the author, but as a thought it belongs to the human race'.[34] The Enlightenment's 'Republic of Letters' lived on.

The following week, Hugo suffered a stroke. He had noted some memory loss three years earlier but a period of abstinence from sex had proven to be an effective enough remedy at the time. Recently, he had not shown any such restraint with Blanche. Juliette's earlier warning that he would do well to avoid 'these gusset-sporting tramps who prowl around you like wild dogs' had no effect,[35] but the limits of her patience had been reached now that his health appeared to be at urgent risk. He was persuaded to return to Hauteville House for a restorative vacation with his family. By the time they returned to Paris for the winter, Juliette had successfully pushed Blanche out

Photograph of Hugo with his family and friends at the back of Hauteville House, July 1878. From left to right: Richard Lesclide (Hugo's secretary), Louis Koch (Juliette Drouet's nephew) and his son, Juliette Drouet, Victor Hugo, Jeanne Hugo seated next to him, Julie Chenay (Hugo's sister-in-law), Alice Lockroy (Charles Hugo's widow, remarried to Édouard Lockroy) and her son Georges, Madame Menard-Dorian and her daughter Pauline Menard (later wife of Georges Hugo).

of his life in order to remove deadly temptation. They were to live next door to Alice and her family in a house on the Avenue d'Eylau in the tranquil and affluent sixteenth arrondissement. A carriage was purchased to try and stop him from travelling on the Parisian omnibus to attend or arrange rendezvous with the opposite sex. His loved ones thrust seemliness upon him.

Hugo's stride became more hesitant, his mood was uncharacteristically irritable, his hearing worsened and he was no longer an early riser. However, he still managed to escape the decorum that had been thrust upon him and privately meet with women by intermittently slipping away from the family home. Up until just shy of two months before his death, his diary continued to log coded entries that lend themselves to a sexual interpretation.[36] He also continued to socialize and make public appearances, the last of which came late in 1884 when he visited Frédéric Bartholdi's workshop to see the Statue of Liberty that the Republic would gift to the United States (one woman he did not need to visit in private). But he would never again put together a complete literary work. The strokes of his pen greatly slowed and his writing became much more sporadic and fragmented. Revivals of his plays proved ever popular. The new titles that appeared in bookstores over the next seven years came from his backlog of writing, which was edited for publication by Vacquerie and Meurice (whom he had earlier named as executors in his will). Thematically and stylistically, they revealed little that could not have been gleaned from his previous works, but they often succeeded in engaging his voice with current affairs.

In 1879, the first of three long poems, *Supreme Pity*, pleaded for forgiveness towards perpetrators of political violence as 'those defined by blindness, fury, and the dark night'.[37] *Religions and Religion* and *The Ass* followed in 1880. The former revisited Hugo's philosophy of God as an inestimable divine force that was too prodigious to sit still on the altars of religious institutions ('He is! Without an end, a dawn,/ Without eclipse or night, without repose or sleep').[38] The latter was a more satirical poem which, like *Supreme Pity*, had been written in the late 1850s for the abandoned section on the nineteenth century in *The Legend of the Ages*. As in English, 'ass' has a double meaning of 'fool' and 'donkey' which divides between the poem's two main figures. The German philosopher Immanuel Kant listens to a wise donkey called Patience, who mocks empirical reason for discrediting God on the basis that it cannot figure out the divine's mysteries. 'Before this luminous, enormous enigma,/ Its eye invisible, its hands impalpable,/ Science zigzags between answers, incapable.'[39] Together, the two poems amplified Hugo's call for a spirit of enquiry in thought and education, free from religious dogma and intellectual superiority.

All three works made him appear in sync with the republicans' firmer hold on French politics. In July 1880, the campaign for a complete amnesty to be granted to the Communards succeeded and was the subject of his last speech to the Senate. The amnesty came in time for the 14 July celebrations, which the government had declared to be a national holiday. The French Revolution was now accorded the status of modern France's founding moment, in line with Hugo's vision of history. Furthermore, over the next two years the Jules Ferry Laws made education free, compulsory and secular. The Third Republic's efforts to integrate the country's difficult past into a more coherent national identity and to expand its civic powers put the arguments that Hugo had been making for years into practice.

He had become a legitimizing example for the republican factions in the Assembly. Selections from his oeuvre would be included in the national syllabus and his birthday on 26 February 1881 was marked by a weekend of festivities that ended with a huge procession. Braving the cold weather, half a million people passed his house and cried 'Vive la France! Vive Victor Hugo!' The 'poet patriot', as one journalist described him, looked on, teary-eyed, with his family. He received 2,000 telegrams from all over the world and a standing ovation in the Senate several days later, and the Avenue d'Eylau was renamed the Avenue Victor-Hugo in his honour. These homages celebrated Hugo entering his eighth decade, since he was still a year away from turning eighty. This less-than-elegant logic hinted that the Republic wanted to capitalize on his aura sooner rather than later, just in case.

The publication of three additional works between 1881 and 1883 gave the impression that the haste was unnecessary. *The Four Winds of the Spirit* offered an anthology of previously unseen verse divided into a quartet of moods – satiric, dramatic (a pair of short plays), lyric and epic – as he had intended. Each represented his conception of the modern poet as 'judge, pastor, prophet, and apostle' for whom the path to self-understanding was still an incomplete learning curve: 'Nobody but myself knows my abyss./ And have I ever plumbed its depths?'[40] *Torquemada*, a play dramatizing religious repression, was published in 1882 when the Russian pogroms gathered pace after the assassination of Tsar Alexander II. Finally, the third and last cycle of *The Legend of the Ages* was released in 1883.

In the month prior to its publication, however, Hugo lost his most loyal audience. On 11 May, Juliette died after a long battle with stomach cancer. She had asked him to 'be patient with my incessant and frequent pain and rally me to live through lots of love', but his willing attempts had failed.[41] The constancy of her companionship, devotion and ability to forgive was gone. He had written years earlier that 'to be loved is to be useful' and that 'the day when no one loves me anymore, oh God, I hope I will die'.[42] Inconsolable and stunned, he locked himself away in his bedroom. He was unable to attend the funeral or confront his grief through his writing, as he had so often done in the past. A diary entry promising that he would only be apart from Juliette temporarily proved to be his last prophetic act.

In May 1885, Hugo fell ill with pneumonia. Over the following week, his diagnosis made international headlines and a crowd of 5,000 assembled outside his Paris town house. Hugo was finally bidding adieu after watching over France's nascent Third Republic at the end of a distinctly long and eventful life. On the afternoon of 22 May he died at the age of 83. From his deathbed, he had pronounced a perfect alexandrine about the struggle between day and night and claimed to see 'black light'. The frail barque that was unable to drop anchor had taken to new waters.

The Hour – real or calamitous –
Raises its mystifying brow.
Well, I'm not worried, anyhow;
I always have been curious.[43]

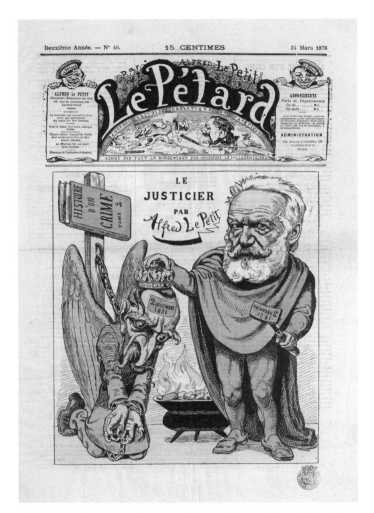

Alfred Le Petit, 'Victor Hugo, the Justiciary', *Le Pétard*, 24 March 1878, lithograph on the second volume of *History of a Crime*. Hugo, upright and in classical garb, brands the fallen emperor (depicted as an imperial eagle) with the mark of 2 December 1851 for the *coup d'état*.

6

'I will be closing my eyes, but . . .'
(Post-1885)

'. . . my inner eye will remain more open than ever.' This chapter title's declaration, taken from Hugo's will, testifies to his belief that the grave was a luminous doorway to an unrivalled outlook.[1] For Hugo, his death would see him transition between the two planes of existence: the earthly, natural and social in the here and now; and the other-worldly, supernatural and spiritual that beckoned beyond that material reality. He had trained himself to see these two interacting levels by exercising both the physical and inner forms of sight, akin to an ancient seer's visionary powers.

When his body succumbed to pneumonia in 1885, the idea of Hugo transcending into an all-seeing mystical state was more inevitable than far-fetched in the minds of many French citizens. His intuitive righteousness during his exile had canonized his persona as one of the Académie française's 'immortals', as if he had already departed this world and accessed a higher standpoint. By the time of his return to Paris in 1870, the excited crowd waiting for him might have been forgiven for thinking that his train would be arriving from the hereafter and that no mere mortal would be stepping onto the platform. One caricature early the following year had depicted an old woman rebuking a young boy for senselessly trying to sell the perennial Hugo a bullet-proof vest during the Prussian siege of Paris ('Imbecile, not for him, Victor Hugo is immortal!');[2] others throughout the 1870s and early 1880s had made use of the prophetic iconography that became popular for signifying

Hugo's unassailable wisdom, including a statuesque body, large forehead, sagacious white beard and classical symbols such as the lyre and white robes.

Hugo's historic funeral in Paris adds the final aspects to this book's portrait of him. Rather than bring his story to an end, this grandiose ceremony can function as another of Hugo's inversions, since it marked the beginning of a new and open-ended chapter in his biography. The idea of taking on new life in death is in keeping with the kind of transformative logic that Hugo preferred. The ceremony itself tellingly dramatized his Romantic world view of opposites drawn into close association and so allows for a summary of his key ideas in this sixth and closing chapter. Furthermore, the funeral cemented Hugo's prestige as one of France's foremost *grands hommes* – the 'great men' (and women) to whom the inscription across the Pantheon's entrance in Paris records the country's debt. This esteem has helped his afterlife to flourish, but it must be approached with some caution so as not to lose sight of Hugo himself.

To the Pantheon

Hugo was an ideal deity for a secular republic that was finding its footing. The Third Republic had been France's sturdiest to date, having already lasted nearly five times as long as the country's previous attempt after the February Revolution of 1848. Nevertheless, its proponents were still trying to manage the sensitive legacy of 1789 and ensure that the country would not be pulled apart by the disputes between monarchists, Bonapartists, republicans and socialists. Hugo exerted a unifying presence within this divisive environment, and the Jules Ferry Laws had already made his work a requisite subject for teaching in the new free non-religious schools. Eschewing political allegiances and pointing to the higher calling of a prosperous future, Hugo was perfectly placed as a founding father who could be commemorated with all the potency of sacred worship, as had been the case during the celebrations for his impending eightieth year in 1881.

Hugo had emphasized an independent spirit as early as his twenties when he had begun to look back on the road he was travelling. He had been aware that such independence could elevate him above factional politics and help him speak to the kind of less partisan, more universal audience envisaged by the French philosophers of the previous century. In a country anxious not to repeat the two extremes of absolute monarchy and Revolutionary Terror, his political sympathies in the first half of the century had evolved from conservative royalism to nostalgic Bonapartism, and then to republican liberalism. Critics had accused him of opportunism, but he was guided by his dedication to French pre-eminence rather than by any deep-seated political affiliation: 'No party has ever been able to confine me; equally, I will never lead one.'[3] His spiritual convictions were no less averse to labels. Republican fears that his lifelong rejection of the Catholic Church might have given way to a deathbed conversion to France's historic faith were ill founded. His poem 'Civil Burials' from the second cycle of *The Legend of the Ages* (1877) outlined that, although he was a man of faith, he would never be a man of the Church. He wanted 'the true light and not the false lustre', dismissing a priest and demanding that 'a senator of the real' eulogize his final journey.[4]

The day after Hugo died, the prime minister Henri Brisson proposed a state funeral that, in effect, required God Himself to stand aside. Hugo would be laid to rest in the Pantheon, which was to be changed from a church to a mausoleum for the distinguished citizens of France, as it had been in the years following the Revolution. The archbishop of Paris, Cardinal Guibert, complained that the sacred site of Saint Geneviève was about to welcome a man who had repeatedly attacked the Church's authority and refused the last rites, but his protests were in vain. The symbolic power of a national funeral had been evidenced by both the British in 1852 for the Duke of Wellington and by the Americans in 1865 for Abraham Lincoln, where each country took advantage of improving communication and transportation networks to draw its population together. As neither a military hero nor a past president, Hugo's place in the national consciousness was more psychological than institutional. Brisson and his ministers were understandably determined to seize this opportunity, knowing that it would help to legitimize the Third Republic while uniting the country in mourning.

Early on Sunday 31 May, Hugo's coffin was taken to a catafalque bearing his initials underneath the Arc de Triomphe, which had been half-veiled in black. The coffin was laid in state amid a mound of wreaths. A celebratory atmosphere took hold that evening, in spite of overnight rainfall. By the next morning, columns of spectators lined the route that had been announced for the funeral procession. The city's working-class districts would be avoided: the fourteenth anniversary of the violent suppression of the Paris Commune had taken place just one week earlier and the government was keen to avoid any unrest for such a high-profile occasion. The procession was to descend the Champs-Élysées, cross the Seine, pass before the Palais Bourbon as the seat of the country's political power, then take the boulevards Saint-Germain and Saint-Michel before reaching the Pantheon. Before it got under way, speeches were delivered from a tribune next to the catafalque: 'This is not a funeral, but an apotheosis,' proclaimed the president of the Chamber of Deputies, Charles Floquet. 'We commend the eternal apostle whose word remains with us.'[5]

Once the speeches had concluded, the *Marseillaise* was played and, at eleven o'clock, a canon salute signalled the ceremony's start. The clouds had cleared. Schools and shops had closed; street-traders sold flowers and mementoes; balconies along the procession route had been rented out, although many spectators had refused the

Photograph of the Arc de Triomphe, half-veiled, as Hugo's coffin lies in state underneath, 1 June 1885.

steep prices and instead found alternative vantage points such as in trees and on roofs. A military regiment led the vanguard as the coffin began its journey in a pauper's hearse, as per Hugo's wishes. The funeral cortège, comprising Hugo's family, members of the Académie française, the diplomatic corps and the French Court of Cassation, was followed by over three hundred delegations from France, its overseas territories and her allies, as well a further six hundred different groups, from workers unions to artistic associations. An estimated one million francs was spent on flowers alone. A procession of 100,000 mourners made their way through a mass of onlookers that was thought to be made up of at least two million people (equalling, if not outnumbering, the population of Paris).

Proceedings lasted until the early evening, when the final salute occurred in front of the Pantheon. Friedrich Nietzsche – not a great fan of the writer he later described as the 'Pharos at the sea of nonsense' – derided the funeral as 'a veritable orgy of bad taste combined with self-admiration',[6] but it was the mix of public grief and national solidarity that the government had wanted. Parallels include funerals for the Taiwanese President Chiang Ching-kuo in 1988 (attended by over a million mourners in Taipei), for Diana, Princess of Wales in 1997 (which saw over a million people line the route of the cortège in London) and for Pope John Paul II in 2005 (when four million people mourned together in Rome). Even by these modern standards, it remains one of history's most extraordinary public funerals.

Death as a Doorway

Even though Hugo was not responsible for the planning of his funeral ceremony, the monarch of Romantic melodrama had still created one of his most memorable disparities for this final act. He had perhaps anticipated the *London Evening Standard*'s assessment on 2 June of 'a pageant which, though nominally in honour of Victor Hugo, partook rather of the character of a parade, or self-manifestation of the new Democratic regime'. The pauper's hearse that he had chosen stood out against the wider spectacle that France had previously only seen afforded to royal or imperial figures.

Hugo's unusual choice of funeral carriage offers a useful reminder of why he had become such a fabled personality. The vivid sight of sobriety among pageantry as the pauper's hearse made its journey through the streets of Paris was not just the work of an opportune self-promoter, but also of a meditative artist making a statement from beyond the grave. The 1885 ceremony was a marriage of greatness and humility, in which the distance between magnificence and meekness could be challenged. Just as Hugo's philosophy found correspondences between the ostensibly divided worlds of mortal and immortal being, so too did his funeral convey his belief that the commonality of all life and humankind was its source of lasting majesty.

Hugo had been born into a century in which the divine right of kings had been exposed as man's invention rather than God's will, and into a society in which the past was increasingly present and unsettled in the fallout from the French Revolution. He therefore had little difficulty focusing his eyes upon his world's changeability as evidence of its true nature. Looking at – and then past – initial appearance, he could focus on reality and, at the same time, expand his perspective to access the more far-reaching vista hinted at in his will. By probing beneath the surface of things through this combination of sight and insight, he not only painted the world as it appeared to him, he also sketched a cosmic truth – a vision in which this universe and everything within it was bound together through the same infinite and cascading process of creation. 'Do not say: to die; say: to be born', one poem advised, before observing a new dawn over the burial place, in whose light the

The pauper's hearse makes its way through Paris, carrying Hugo's body to the Pantheon, 1 June 1885.

dreadful is revealed to be angelic.[7] From such a stance, death is life, and life is death.

Therein lay a less momentary, more enduring truth beyond history's tumult that greatly enhanced Hugo's appeal as a modern-day visionary. The real power in this world did not yield before altars and thrones, nor did it reside within political parties or measure itself in material wealth and military strength. The only truly sovereign force Hugo discerned was the inexhaustible creative power at the heart of all life: a universal energy driving the ebb and flow of nature and history. This transience was, for him, the hallmark of a mysterious divine creation: 'a God who would not understand much from sermons, schemata, or missals',[8] given that this immeasurable divinity exceeded the capacities of human reason. Humanity could never know God, in the sense of a full and comprehensive understanding, so its usual bearers of knowledge such as the priest, the philosopher and the scientist were limited in the meanings they could give to life's enigmas.

In contrast, Hugo claimed that the creativity of a free and poetically inspired mind could relate more profoundly to God's endless vigour. It did so by seeing points of contact in moments of rupture and by imagining voids like death to be full of possibility. Recounting how starlight coruscates through the black of night, he wrote: 'It's especially at night that we see the suns above; it's especially in exile that we see the homeland; it's especially in the grave that we see God.'[9] By attuning his senses to this natural order of cycles and metamorphoses, Hugo wanted to bring human intelligence and innovation into a closer and more fertile relationship with the world. Without this synchrony with life's inherent openness and indeterminism, he foresaw an abortive future that would always be held back by short-sightedness and narrow-mindedness.

Crucial to the public outpouring of affection at his funeral was the appreciation of moral duty that he nurtured in this role

Bishop Myriel (Cedric Hardwicke) gives Jean Valjean (Fredric March) his silver candlesticks in *Les Misérables* (dir. Richard Boleslawski, 1935). The Hollywood film, also starring Charles Laughton as Javert, was nominated for Best Picture and Best Film Editing at that year's Academy Awards.

of an oracle communing with a higher truth. He knew that his Romantic sensibility would only be relevant if his readers were able to recognize their own everyday experiences in what he wrote. If he strained his eyes to look into the unknown, he also kept his feet on solid ground and refocused on the immediate world around him: 'Show me your foot, genius, and let us see if you, like me, have earth on your heel.'[10] He had no patience with utilitarian conceptions of art that considered the writer simply to fulfil a social function, nor could he abide the credos of 'art for art's sake': the former confined the artist to this world alone, whereas the latter sanctioned a permanent flight away from it. In Hugo's eyes, any artist seeking truth had to commit to freeing both art and society from rigid structures and fixed ideas, and in particular to opposing injustice and repression wherever they threatened the autonomy of creation. The value of art and of the human individual as agents of progress could not be underestimated.

He optimized that value by promoting greater freedom of expression and self-realization. Categorical thinking that partitioned life into clear-cut meanings with hard and fast edges could not make real sense of a creative world. Divisions and limitations, whether aesthetic or social, needed to be seen in more organic terms as porous or unfixed lines of separation so as to harbour rather than inhibit growth. The most famous of his literary heroes – the ex-convict Jean Valjean and the hunchbacked bell-ringer Quasimodo – both illustrate this principle of conversion: that the supposedly insignificant and marginalized among us are central to a more meaningful world, and that the physically or morally monstrous can also be honourable. Conversely, those heroes' antagonists – the police inspector Javert and Notre-Dame's archdeacon, Claude Frollo

Esmeralda (Patsy Ruth Miller) offers Quasimodo (Lon Chaney) water during his flogging in *The Hunchback of Notre-Dame* (dir. Wallace Worsley, 1923).

– typify how pure and lawful souls can still be wicked and inhuman: 'all the bad of good'.[11] The more rigid a character is in Hugo's writing, the more twisted and degraded they become; the more pliable and fluid they are, the more upright they seem. He thereby warns his readers against what happens when dogma and zeal win out over openness and compassion. Since 'there can be nothing truly infallible in a human being',[12] humanity's moral worth is reckoned not in absolutist terms, but in what we make of our imperfections in a life that is transitory rather than perfectible.

In this respect, the 1885 funeral's dual performance of modesty and stateliness confirmed Hugo's proclivity for grand gestures, but with the same stroke it reiterated his need to remain connected with the everyday. Even though he yearned to be a man apart and above, soaring atop the summits of Olympus or Sinai, he also fretted that such altitudes were neither sustainable nor desirable. He feared he would fall short of these heights yet welcomed such descent as the chance to reconnect with all that mortal existence had to offer. The oscillation between brilliance and reticence, the godly and the human, was forever in play and gave his work its main source of drama.

The Poet as Monument and as Commodity

Keeping those tensions alive is not easy, however, under the weight of Hugo's reputation. In death, he took on new life. His entourage helped to confect his legend through posthumous publications and testimonies, as did the sculptor Auguste Rodin's monuments to him. This renown can cast a distorted shadow of his life and work as much as reveal his shape and depth. Having achieved godlike stature even before he died, the posthumous Hugo risked turning into the remote prophet he had warned against. Sanctified on the pedestal of popular adulation, and with the clichés of greatness and patriarchal authority firmly riveted to his frame, he had become the kind of imposing national monument that is admired or scorned from afar, rather than one to be looked at more closely.

Such scrutiny became all the trickier in the emerging mass market of modern celebrity, which privileged his image over his substance. His likeness adorned a profusion of souvenirs and merchandise. Subsequent celebrations to mark the 1902 centenary of his birth bolstered the Hugo brand with calendars, collectors' coins, confectionery, inkwells, playing cards, stamps, statuettes, tableware and tobacco boxes. Among other centenary festivities, a new museum was opened at the house in the Place des Vosges where he had lived for most of the 1830s and '40s, and Louis-Ernest Barrias' bronze monument was unveiled at the Place Victor-Hugo. Whether his compatriots liked him or not, and despite feelings of 'Hugolatry' and 'Hugophobia' becoming progressively more polarized, the consensus decreed that his importance in French history was inexorable. It prompted André Gide's notorious (if perhaps misunderstood) 'alas!' that same year when he picked Hugo as the greatest poet of nineteenth-century France.

The result of this deification is that, through the next century and beyond, Hugo could be seen everywhere and anywhere, but more as an idea or idol. In the 1920s, the Vietnamese religion of Cao Dai made him one of its saints. The Victor Hugo who overlooked France's commemorations of the 1985 centenary of his death and the 2002 bicentenary of his birth conjured a more secular but no less mythic presence. The complexities of his writing and his character can unsurprisingly be levelled out by this idealized image of the incomparable *grand homme*.

The complete extent of his global afterlife in popular and political culture would be tremendously difficult to ascertain. Artists and political leaders within and beyond France have repeatedly been able to speak through him, adapting and appropriating his words in line with their own creativity and aspirations. His work has been

Marius (Eddie Redmayne), Enjolras (Aaron Tveit) and the ABCs prepare
for insurrection in the award-winning film musical of Boublil and Schönberg's
Les Misérables (dir. Tom Hooper, 2012).

retold in myriad forms, from Hollywood film and European radio
to Japanese manga comics and international musical theatre and
opera. The eclectic list of producers and performers who have been
drawn into this continually growing body of adaptations – from
Walt Disney Studios to Orson Welles – underlines the universal
nature of Hugo's appeal. Likewise, his social beliefs have been cited
by Martin Luther King, Hugo Chávez and Manmohan Singh, to
name but a few.

More recently, candidates running in all three of the new
millennium's presidential elections in France thus far have invoked
his name, maximizing his flexibility as at once the Republic's fiercest
critic and its proudest champion. In the run-up to his 2017 election
victory, Emmanuel Macron chose Hugo as his historical hero,
describing him as 'the reference point we turn to when we want to
rise above ourselves' towards a more creative and magnanimous
society. Macron was harnessing Hugo's unifying potential for his

own centrist position, just two years after separate national polls had confirmed Hugo as the country's writer of choice.[13]

What is clear from such ubiquity is that Hugo has secured the posterity he eyed up. The length and breadth of that wide-ranging history makes it difficult, however, to focus in on what he himself actually wrote and said. That difficulty is compounded by his heady combination of humanitarianism and bravura, which lacks sense if it is not tempered with the more grounded viewpoints that he sought for himself. When dealing with a writer who exhibits the kind of influence and imaginative flair that Hugo does, it is hard not to approach him retrospectively and from a distance as the 'great man', but to do so opens the way either to astonishment at best or bewilderment (if not outright scepticism) at worst. Hugo's name may return more Google hit results than those of Jane Austen and Mark Twain combined (in a total that far surpasses tallies for nineteenth-century French writers such as Honoré de Balzac and Jules Verne),[14] but this span does not guarantee direct or lucid access to its subject.

That is not to say that the posthumous Hugo should either be taken for granted or briskly rebutted. To be sure, there are many exciting networks of reception to explore, each of which highlights the processes through which writers like him travel and translate across different eras, media and cultures. Too often, biographers and critics have, for example, discredited the adaptations of his work as derivative imitations, rather than considered them as part of a frequently inventive history that brings new volume to his voice. His afterlife secures his place in contemporary culture and adds value to how we understand the status of writers as cultural artefacts. Nonetheless, this immensity of reputation and its capacity to rouse the emotions does create ever-larger silhouettes of Hugo that make it harder to grasp his actual human figure.

The tagline for the 2010 London cast recording for the 25th anniversary of *Les Miz* may have tantalizingly encouraged audiences to 'dream the dream', but Hugo emphasized that 'the dreamer has to be stronger than the dream' and not lose themselves in fantasy.[15] For Hugo, being in the moment while being transported elsewhere called for resilience. No discussion of Hugo can bypass his renown, given that it is both an ambition he fostered and a fact of his success, but neither should any chronicle be preoccupied with that fame. To tell his story means neither idealizing nor stigmatizing the man through the myth.

Conclusion

Following Hugo's death, Meurice oversaw a series of posthumous publications that harvested various fragments from his close friend's unpublished writing, as if he was still alive. These included his unseen theatrical works, journals, letters, philosophical essays and travel writing, as well as the verse poems of *The End of Satan* (1886), *The Whole Lyre* (1888–97), *God* (1891), *The Fateful Years* (1898) and *The Last Gleaning* (1902). The impression that he was speaking from beyond the grave enhanced the immortality of Hugo's persona and of his 'deeds and words'.

We can only speculate as to what he might have made of the twenty-first century. How would the defender of *Les Misérables* have responded to the ever-widening differentials in wealth distribution across the world and to persistent gender inequality? How would the outspoken writer with a vivid imagination and virile sex drive have fared in the age of social media, digital technology and online pornography? And what would the poet who found repose in nature have felt about the ecological and environmental issues that the planet faces? Looking to him for firm answers to such questions, however, risks making him speak out of context. He becomes either a source of impeccably timeless wisdom or a fountain of obsolete and uninitiated thinking. Neither characterization is fluid enough for the posterity he envisaged.

On 10 January 2016, at the Place de le République, Hugo's speech of 5 September 1870 was read out at a ceremony in which the city of

Paris mourned those 147 lives that had been lost in the 2015 terrorist attacks. The patriot returning to a country under siege offered solidarity: 'Whoever attacks Paris attacks the whole human race . . . Paris will triumph . . . Snuff out all hatred, be done with all resentment, be united.'[1] His defiance resonated with a grieving country that felt its republican values under extreme threat.

The following year, a student in Martinique launched a petition to be sent to the French Education Ministry. She asked that 'French teachers learn and teach that Victor Hugo was also a racist'.[2] The petition referred to Hugo's 1879 speech on Africa at a commemoration event for the abolition of slavery, in which he encouraged France's colonial expansion. 'In the twentieth century, Europe will make Africa into a world,' he declared. 'God offers Africa to Europe. Take it. Where kings would bring war, bring unity . . . not in the name of conquest, but for brotherhood.'[3] On the cusp of the 'Scramble for Africa', his speech smacked of the 'civilizing mission' of European countries like France to enlighten the world's benighted corners.

These cases presented two very different Hugos: a champion of the Republic's will to rise above division, and an advocate of its apparent implicit bias towards white Europeans. With both, the clichés of the *grand homme* left no room for Hugo's more sinuous character. The cultural and racial dimensions of these two examples call for more insight and nuance than the polished, hard edges of the many monuments to him allow. Hugo does not have to be read in his entirety, but an illustrative idea of who he was and what he believed is still necessary to resist the grip of stereotypes and to avoid parroting or clipping what he said. His claim during exile that all his works needed to be read together if he was to be understood is more a sign of his insecurity than any realistic expectation, especially given the exchanges in his writing between the particular and the general.[4] The part gives access to the whole, but only if its context is inclusive enough. The image of a republican lion or an insidious racist sheds scant light on a writer who decried both the

Communards and the *Versaillais*, or on the pacifist who spoke out against slavery and state-sanctioned aggression.

The awkwardness of Hugo's support for the *mission civilisatrice* should neither be misrepresented nor disregarded. The author of *Bug-Jargal* evidently did not believe that skin colour predestined any individual to physical or intellectual superiority. Kinship superseded genetics: 'What do the two differences in colour matter,' he asked, 'if the pale face and the black face are lit by the same bright dawn of brotherhood?'[5] Notwithstanding this humanitarian stance, he could not resolve the inherent conflict in republican ideology between universalism and difference. He viewed post-Revolutionary France as having a messianic responsibility to use advances in science and the history of ideas as tools for building a fairer, more flourishing world. It was one of his most naively optimistic perspectives, conceitedly exalting the economic and socio-cultural benefits of Western modernity while imagining that colonization could be a non-violent and philanthropic process. This viewpoint was also steeped in a broad cultural ignorance of Africa's rich indigenous history. Inheriting from Renaissance humanism, nineteenth-century Europe had fashioned a Hegelian idea of Africa as a 'dark continent' of primitive cultures that needed illumination.

If, like so many of his contemporaries, Hugo knew nothing of pre-colonial Africa, he knew all too much about his own continent and the human nature that it revealed. His sweeping idealism could not quell his despair at Europe's failure to meet its own civilized standards, either at home or abroad. His ideal was to rid the world of repression – be that from princes or priests, from dictators or dogmatic superstition – and create participatory democracies in which every generation was guaranteed a free-minded education and equality of opportunity. It was a theory that seemed to him to be far from the minds of Europe's political leaders, for whom socio-economic exploitation through military violence won out over shared and peaceful prosperity. 'France is to Africa what England is to Asia,' he wrote ten years before his speech, 'a bad tutor.'[6]

Colonialism teases out the contradictions of Hugo's belief in the republican dream of 1789. His dedication to the *mission civilisatrice* as a providential duty was thwarted by his hostility towards suffering and by his Romantic nostalgia for natural harmony. That tension is evident in the fact that his most direct critiques of colonialism are to be found in the volumes that appeared after his death. While alive, his efforts to unite the republican movement discouraged him from launching overt attacks, although his concerns were intense enough to burst to the surface in various published works.[7] Arguments arose in *Châtiments*, for example, that colonization hardened and dehumanized the French army by engendering a barbarity that risked being mustered against France's own people. Like his disappointment with colonialism's reality, the parallels between his country's subjugation of overseas territories and domestic social oppression became more explicit in his posthumous work. In one such poem, as he looked from the Andes to the Himalayas, he scorned the self-interest of his fellow Europeans: 'You believe you're civilizing a world/ When you're infecting it with some filthy fever,' poisoning Edenic lands with a thirst for gold and warfare.[8] It was a mockery of what he believed progress should look like.

Being one of France's 'great' (white) men might always see Hugo idolized and vilified, but such absolutism ignores his mind's unsettled nature and its dynamic implications. The 2017 petition was not the first time that students have disliked the French education system's reverence towards him, although the discussion it provoked around how historical figures like him cannot be taught in reductive ways remains urgent.[9] Less mythic, more objective approaches to his life and work can read him attentively without glorifying or dismissing the importance of what he accomplished during his lifetime. The result of such approaches might best be summed up by the novelist Gustave Flaubert, who after meeting Hugo for the first time in 1872 wrote that he was 'not at all the great man, not at all pontificating'.[10]

This biography has argued that unqualified or unequivocal answers are simply not forthcoming from Hugo. The unease and ambiguities of his thinking should not be downplayed. They reveal the 'storm on the brain' that Jean Valjean must endure, and that Hugo saw as vital to what it means to be human.

Abbreviations and References

Referencing an *oeuvre* as extensive as Hugo's can be complicated, but my priority has been to help the reader access this large body of work for themselves wherever possible.

Where I have translated Hugo into English myself, the references have been taken primarily from the Ollendorff and Albin Michel 45-volume edition of his complete works (*Œuvres complètes*). This edition can be accessed both at the Bibliothèque nationale de France's digital library, Gallica (https://gallica.bnf.fr), and at the French Wikisource site for Hugo (https://fr.wikisource.org/wiki/Auteur:Victor_Hugo).

The following French titles and abbreviations have been used to indicate the relevant sources from the Ollendorff/Albin Michel volumes:

AP	*Actes et paroles* (Deeds and Words), 3 vols
CRP	*Correspondance* (Correspondence), 4 vols
CV	*Choses vues* (Things Seen), 2 vols
Hst	*Histoire* (History), 2 vols
OB	*Odes et ballades* (Odes and Ballads), *Pse* I
Phil	*Philosophie* (Philosophy), 2 vols
Pse	*Poésie* (Poetry), 15 vols
Rom	*Roman* (Novels), 9 vols
Tht	*Théâtre* (Theatre), 6 vols

Some references were taken from other sources, as follows:

CV (Juin)   *Choses vues*
             A yet more comprehensive edition of *Choses vues*,
             ed. Hubert Juin, 2 vols (Paris, 1972)

JD	Letters from Juliette Drouet to Victor Hugo
	These letters can be consulted at the ever-expanding archives at www.juliettedrouet.org (ed. Florence Naugrette); no page numbers are included since the letters can be accessed by a search engine
OC (Laffont)	*Œuvres complètes*
	The more recent (and reorganized) eighteen-volume Robert Laffont edition of Hugo's complete works, with specific reference to vols XI (*Histoire*), XIII (*Voyages*) and XV (*Océan*)

Where existing English translations of Victor Hugo's fiction and poetry have been used, these references are indicated by the following abbreviations:

BJ	*Bug-Jargal*, trans. Chris Bongie (Peterborough, ON, 2004)
EVH	*The Essential Victor Hugo*, trans. E. H. and A. M. Blackmore (Oxford, 2004)
Mis	*Les Misérables*, trans. Julie Rose (London, 2008)
NDP	*Notre-Dame de Paris*, trans. John Sturrock (London, 2004)
SP	*Selected Poems of Victor Hugo*: a Bilingual Edition, trans. E. H. and A. M. Blackmore (Chicago, IL, 2001)
TS	*The Toilers of the Sea*, trans. James Hogarth (New York, 2002)

For *EVH* and *SP*, I have also included in the relevant endnotes the name of the collection from which the poem is taken (if this is not clear from the main text) and/or its sequence number. This supplemental information will allow the poems to be easily tracked in other editions.

Introduction

1 *William Shakespeare, Phil* II, p. 181.

2 The moniker 'immortal' comes from the motto 'To Immortality' on the Académie's official seal.

3 Hugo's correspondence reveals a lingering concern with his eyes that began in the mid-1820s with severe inflammation. He appears to have suffered from hyperlacrimation (excess tear production), aggravated by moments of stress and in part leading to corneal ulcers in late 1829. His intensive work regime, including extended periods of late-night writing, did not help, nor did his love of setting suns. He told Franz Liszt in a letter dated 15 June 1834 that 'sometimes I think I will go blind' (*CRP* I, p. 542). His doctor recommended that he wear tinted lenses when outdoors, as well as walk through green areas such as public parks to reduce eye strain; see Jean-Marc Hovasse, *Victor Hugo, avant l'exil 1802–51* (Paris, 2001), pp. 214–15, 419–20 and 539, as well as his essay 'La vue de Victor Hugo', in *L'Œil de Victor Hugo*, ed. Pierre Georgel et al. (Paris, 2004), pp. 3–25.

4 Jean Cocteau, *Essai de critique indirecte: le mystère laïc* (Paris, 1932), p. 28.

5 *Les Travailleurs de la mer*, *Rom* VII, p. 326.

6 'On vit, on parle . . .' (*Contemplations* IV, xi), *Pse* III, p. 232.

7 Some chapters in Hugo's life have been retold in various ways. The story of his marriage in the early 1830s formed the backdrop for Helen Humphreys's novel *The Reinvention of Love* (2011); his political activism and stormy private life during the French Second Republic became the subject of a mini-series called *Victor Hugo, ennemi d'État* (2018), directed by Jean-Marc Moutout and produced by the national television channel France 2; and his exile was the focus both for M. J. Rose's novel *Seduction* (2013) and Esther Gil and Laurent Paturaud's graphic novel *Victor Hugo, aux frontières de l'exil* (2013). His youngest daughter was also at the centre of François Truffaut's award-winning 1975 film *The Story of Adèle H.*

8 For the central example of this adaptive legacy, see Kathryn M. Grossman and Bradley Stephens, eds, *Les Misérables and its Afterlives: Between Page, Stage, and Screen* (London, 2015).

9 In French, Alain Decaux's near thousand-page work is a standout (1984); the most recent was Sandrine Fillipetti's 368-page book

(2011). Substantial English-language biographies over three hundred pages long were published by Joanna Richardson in 1976 (which is unnecessarily subjective in parts), and by both A. F. Davidson in 1912 and Elliott M. Grant in 1945 (which are now somewhat outdated). See Bibliography for details.

10   Aside from translations of most of Hugo's fiction and some anthologies of his poetry, general English introductions are available in John Andrew Frey's *A Victor Hugo Encyclopaedia* (Westport, CT, 1999) and in Marva Barnett's *Victor Hugo on Things that Matter* (New Haven, CT, 2009). Both are reference studies rather than extensive analyses, helpfully grouping samples of Hugo's writing under various headings. Frey's compendium runs to over three hundred pages; Barnett's more topical organization is over four hundred pages long but does not include English translations of Hugo's French. Laurence M. Porter's study *Victor Hugo* (Boston, MA, 1999) translates its many references, but Porter's otherwise deep focus curiously begins to close around the late exile period. A more integrated resource for anglophone readers could copy or abridge any of the French editions of Hugo's complete works. It would be especially helpful in opening up Hugo's theatre, political writing and critical thinking to a non-French audience.

11   Marie-Laure Prévost, *Le Cahier 'Victor Hugo, l'homme océan'* (Paris, 2002), p. 2.

12   *William Shakespeare*, *Phil* II, pp. 93–4.

13   *CV* (Juin), I, p. 368.

14   *OC* (Laffont) XV, p. 298.

15   'To Algernon Charles Swinburne', *CRP*, 14 July 1869.

16   *William Shakespeare*, *Phil* II, p. 627.

17   'Que nous avons le doute en nous' (*Les Chants du crépuscule*, xxxviii), *Pse* II, p. 304.

18   See Baudelaire's preface to his translations of Edgar Allan Poe's *Extraordinary Tales*: *Œuvres completes*, vol. I (Paris, 1975), p. 709.

19   These descriptions were recorded by the publisher Pierre-Jules Hetzel when he watched Hugo swimming in September 1857, and the poet Théodore de Banville at the *Les Misérables* banquet on 16 September 1862: A. Parménie and C. Bonnier de la Chapelle, *Histoire d'un éditeur et ses auteurs: Hetzel* (Paris, 1985), p. 274; and Banville, *Critique littéraire, artistique, et musicale choisie*, vol. II (Paris, 2004), p. 67.

1 'I want to be Chateaubriand or nothing' (1802–22)

1 See Charles Baudouin, *Psychanalyse de Victor Hugo* [1943], ed. Pierre Albouy (Paris, 1972), pp. 132–7.

2 'Ce qui se passait aux Feuillantines, vers 1813' (*Les Rayons et les ombres*, xix), *Pse* II, p. 590.

3 Jean-Marc Hovasse, *Victor Hugo, avant l'exil 1802–51* (Paris, 2001), p. 76.

4 *OC* (Laffont) XIII, p. 763.

5 Cited in Graham Robb, *Victor Hugo* (London, 1997), p. 32.

6 'À M. de Chateaubriand', *OB* (III, ii), p. 138.

7 Hugo used this salutation in much of his correspondence with his mother.

8 'To General Hugo', 22 June and 12 November 1816, *CRP* I, pp. 293–5.

9 'Le rétablissement de la statue de Henri IV', *OB* (I, vi), p. 64.

10 Cited in Florence Naugrette, *Le Théâtre de Victor Hugo* (Lausanne, 2016), pp. 7–8.

11 'To Adolphe Trébuchet', 21 September 1820, *CRP* I, pp. 316–17.

12 'Le poète dans les révolutions', *OB* (I, i), p. 40.

13 'To General Hugo', 28 June 1821, *CRP* I, p. 322.

14 'To Pierre Foucher', 3 August 1821, *CRP* I, p. 331.

15 Preface (1822), *OB*, p. 5.

16 Henri Guillemin, *Hugo et la sexualité* (Paris, 1954), pp. 13–14.

17 'To General Hugo', 27 June 1823, *CRP* I, p. 371.

18 'To Adèle Foucher', 19 February 1820 and 21/29 December 1821, *CRP* I, pp. 14, 85 and 90.

2 'I am a force in motion!' (1823–35)

1 *Hernani* (III, iv), *Tht* I, p. 585.

2 *CV* (Juin), I, p. 108.

3 Unknown recipient, dated 1845, *CRP* I, p. 625.

4 'Encore à toi', *OB* (v, xii), p. 261.

5 'La Mort de Mademoiselle de Sombreuil', *OB* (II, ix), p. 127.

6 'À l'ombre d'un enfant', *OB* (v, xvi), p. 271.

7 *Littérature et philosophie mêlées*, *Phil* I, pp. 116–22.

8   For Hugo's original article, see Jules Marsan, ed., *La Muse française 1823–24* (Paris, 1907), p. 33.

9   See Jean-Marc Hovasse, *Victor Hugo, avant l'exil 1802–51* (Paris, 2001), pp. 277–8.

10 *BJ*, p. 163.

11 'À M. Alphonse de L', *OB* (III, i), p. 137.

12 Preface [1826], *OB*, p. 26.

13 'À la colonne de la Place Vendôme', *OB* (III, vii), p. 172.

14 Théophile Gautier, *Histoire du Romantisme* (Paris, 1874), p. 5.

15 Preface, *Cromwell*, *Tht* I, p. 15.

16 Ibid., p. 45.

17 Ibid., p. 23.

18 Ibid., p. 31.

19 'To Victor Pavie', 29 February 1828, *CRP* I, p. 446.

20 Muhammad Ali Pasha (1769–1849) was an Ottoman Albanian ruler who founded modern Egypt with a Bonaparte-like reputation for modernization and law enforcement.

21 See, for example, Ève Morisi, 'Putting Pain to Paper: Victor Hugo's New Abolitionist Poetics', in *Death Sentences: Literature and State Killing*, ed. Birte Christ and Ève Morisi (Oxford, 2019).

22 *Le Dernier jour d'un condamné*, *Rom* I, pp. 633–4.

23 'To Paul Lacroix', 27 February 1830, *CRP* I, p. 467.

24 'To Adolphe de Saint-Valry', 7 August 1830, *CRP* I, p. 476.

25 'To Sainte-Beuve', 12 June 1832, *CRP* I, p. 509.

26 'Dicté après Juillet 1830', *Les Chants du crépuscule* (i), *Pse* II, p. 185.

27 *NDP*, p. 372.

28 Ibid., pp. 127–9.

29 Ibid., p. 153.

30 Jules Michelet, *Histoire de France* [1837], ebook (Paris, 2016), III/4, ch. VIII.

31 17 July 1831, *CRP* I, p. 497.

32 Preface, *Marion de Lorme*, *Tht* II, p. 8.

33 'Bièvre', *Les Feuilles d'automne* (xxxiv), *Pse* II, p. 96.

34 'To Sainte-Beuve', 12 June 1832, *CRP* I, pp. 508–9.

35 22 August 1833, *CRP* I, p. 532.

36 Jean Gaudon, ed., *Victor Hugo: Lettres à Juliette Drouet* (Paris, 1964), p. 5.

37 Ibid., p. 1.

38 *JD*, 10 August 1833.

39 *Littérature et philosophie mêlées*, *Phil* I, p. 119.

40 Ibid, p. 215.

41 *Claude Gueux*, *Rom* I, pp. 764–5.

42 'Envoi des feuilles d'automne' (xviii); 'Que nous avons le doute en nous' (xxxviii), *Les Chants du crépuscule*, *Pse* II, pp. 250 and 305.

3 'I will set my frail barque onto the wrathful waves' (1836–51)

1 *Les Voix intérieures* (xxix), *Pse* II, pp. 460–66.

2 21 May 1837, *CRP* I, p. 553.

3 5 July 1836, cited in Laura el Makki and Guillaume Gallienne, *Un Été avec Victor Hugo* (Paris, 2016), p. 24.

4 *JD*, 14 August 1836.

5 See Gérard Pouchain and Robert Sabourin, *Juliette Drouet, ou 'la dépaysée'* (Paris, 1992), and Bradley Stephens, '*Baisez-moi, belle Juju!* Victor Hugo and the Joy of his Juliette', in *'Joie de vivre' in French Literature and Culture*, ed. Susan Harrow and Timothy Unwin (Amsterdam, 2009), pp. 211–24.

6 'À Olympio', *Les Voix intérieures* (xxx), *Pse* II, p. 472.

7 *Ruy Blas* (II, ii), *Tht* III, p. 375.

8 Albert W. Halsall, *Victor Hugo and the Romantic Drama* (Toronto, 1998), pp. 169–70.

9 *SP*, pp. 94–105 (*Les Rayons et les ombres*, xxxiv).

10 'Discours de réception', 3 June 1841, *AP* I, p. 51.

11 Letter XXXVIII, *OC* (Laffont), XIII, pp. 397–401. The last metaphor is a reference to the biblical book of Ezekiel.

12 1 February 1842, cited in Jean-Marc Hovasse, *Victor Hugo, avant l'exil 1802–51* (Paris, 2001), p. 848.

13 17 February 1843, cited in Stephens, '*Baisez-moi, belle Juju!*', p. 218.

14 10 September 1843, *CRP* I, p. 611.

15 'A Ol.', *Les Voix intérieures* (xii), *Pse* II, p. 415.

16 *OC* (Laffont) XV, p. 491. The French plays on the meanings of 'queue' as a protrusion, such as a tail, stalk, pan handle or – more colloquially – the male member.

17 'L'amour n'est plus (xix); 'Oh! Dis . . .' (xlviii), *Toute la lyre* (VI), *Pse* XIII, pp. 122 and 161.

18 See Henri Guillemin, *Hugo et la sexualité* (Paris, 1954), pp. 49–63.

19 One of the most thought-provoking discussions remains Charles
    Baudouin's psychoanalytical reading, first published in 1943:
    Baudouin, *Psychanalyse de Victor Hugo* (Paris, 1972).

20 See Hovasse's reminders about the need to exercise some objective
    caution in *Victor Hugo avant*, pp. 1001 and 1240.

21 Cited in Gérard Audinet and Vincent Gille, eds, *Éros Hugo: entre pudeur
    et excès*, exh. cat., Maison de Victor Hugo (Paris, 2015), p. 126.

22 Graham Robb, *Victor Hugo* (London, 1997), p. 257.

23 See Hovasse, *Victor Hugo, avant*, pp. 982–91.

24 22 February 1846 and 9 January 1841, *CV* I, pp. 137 and 59–62.

25 'To Pierre Vinçard', 2 July 1841, *CRP* I, p. 586.

26 *OC* (Laffont) XI, p. 1010.

27 24 June 1848, *CRP* I, pp. 638–9.

28 *OC* (Laffont) XI, p. 1058.

29 *Mis*, pp. 961–2.

30 'Misère', 9 July 1849, *AP* I, pp. 163–4.

31 See Marieke Stein, *Victor Hugo, orateur politique* (Paris, 2007),
    especially pp. 369–85.

32 'Liberté de l'enseignement', 15 January 1850, *AP* I, p. 182.

33 'Révision de la Constitution', 17 July 1851, *AP* I, p. 257.

34 *OC* (Laffont) XI, p. 1238.

35 Ibid., p. 1250.

4 'I feel like I am atop life's true summit' (1852–70)

1 *CV* (Juin), II, p. 343, for this reference and the chapter title.

2 'Joyeuse vie', *Châtiments* (III, ix), *Pse* IV, p. 108.

3 'To Mme. Victor Hugo', 5 January 1852, *CRP* II, p. 43.

4 'To Mme. Victor Hugo', 31 December 1851, *CRP* II, p. 38.

5 'To André Van Hasselt', 6 January 1852, *CRP* II, p. 44.

6 'To Madame Victor Hugo', 5 January 1852, *CRP* II, p. 43.

7 *EVH*, p. 243 ('Ultima verba', *Châtiments*, VII, xvi).

8 See Roger Price, *The French Second Empire* (Cambridge, 2002), Part II,
   and Robert Gildea, *Children of the Revolution: The French, 1799–1914*
   (London, 2008), pp. 59–65.

9   *Napoléon le Petit* (III, and VII, i), *Hst* I, pp. 63 and 151.

10 The emperor had been exiled first to Elba (1814) and then to Saint Helena (1815).

11 18 November 1852, *CRP* II, p. 132.

12 'To Noël Parfait', start of May 1853, *CRP* II, p. 151.

13 'Souvenir de la nuit du 4', *Châtiments* (II, iii), *Pse* IV, p. 66.

14 *EVH*, p. 149 (*Châtiments*, V, xiii).

15 Nicole Savy, 'Victus, sed Victor (1852–1862)', in *En collaboration avec le soleil: Victor Hugo, photographies de l'exil*, ed. Françoise Heilbrun and Danielle Molinari (Paris, 1999), pp. 16–39.

16 For a concise account of Hugo's spiritual interests in exile, see Sudhir Hazareesingh, *How the French Think* (London, 2015), pp. 66–70.

17 See John Chambers, *Victor Hugo's Conversations with the Spirit World* (New York, 2008).

18 'To Émile Deschanel', 14 January 1855, *CRP* II, p. 205.

19 *SP*, pp. 200–201 ('Mors', IV, xvi).

20 'Ce que c'est que la mort', *Contemplations* (VI, xxii), *Pse* III, p. 388.

21 *SP*, pp. 163–7 (I, vii).

22 Ibid., pp. 220–21 ('Hélas! Tout est sepulchre . . .', VI, xviii).

23 J. C. Ireson, *Victor Hugo: A Companion to his Poetry* (Oxford, 1997), p. 191.

24 *Contemplations* (VI, xxiii and xxvi), *Pse* III, pp. 395 and 438.

25 'To Victor Schoelcher', 12 January 1857, *CRP* II, pp. 262–3.

26 *SP*, pp. 313–14.

27 Ibid., pp. 528–9 (II, viii).

28 'To Jules Janin', 16 August 1856, *CRP* II, p. 257.

29 Marie, Laura and Jean-Baptiste Hugo, *Hauteville House: Victor Hugo, décorateur* (Paris, 2016), p. 7.

30 Pierre Georgel, *Drawings by Victor Hugo* (London, 1974), p. iii.

31 *Océan* (1854); cited in Henri Guillemin, *Hugo et la sexualité* (Paris, 1954), p. 69.

32 'Le Satyre', *La Légende des siècles* (XXII), *Pse* VI, p. 24.

33 See Guillemin, *Hugo*, pp. 68–82, and Jean-Marc Hovasse's *Victor Hugo, pendant l'exil 1851–64* (Paris, 2008), who tempers more sensationalist accounts, especially pp. 479–81. Neither author is alone in attesting that Hugo also recorded involuntary orgasms, which he attributed to an 'excess of chastity'.

34 *Mis*, p. 825.

35 'L'Amnistie', 18 August 1859, *AP* II, p. 141.

36 'To Alexander Herzen', 25 July 1855, *CRP* II, p. 218.

37 'John Brown', 2 December 1859, *AP* II, p. 144.

38 'To Monsieur Heurtelou', 31 March 1860, *CRP* II, p. 331.

39 For an excellent history of the novel, see David Bellos, *The Novel of the Century: The Extraordinary Adventure of Les Misérables* (London, 2017).

40 'To Albert Lacroix', 13 March 1862, *CRP* II, p. 381.

41 *Mis*, p. 75.

42 See the preface to *The Tragic Muse* [1890] (London, 1995).

43 *Mis*, p. 422.

44 Ibid., p. 47.

45 Ibid., pp. 615–54.

46 Ibid., p. 1084.

47 Ibid., p. 1194.

48 'To Alfred Darcel', 9 May 1858, *CRP* II, p. 279.

49 'To Captain Butler', 25 November 1861, *AP* II, pp. 161–2. This letter was published fifteen years after it had been sent. A bronze bust of Hugo was unveiled in the old palace for the 150th anniversary in 2010.

50 'La Guerre du Mexique', 1863, *AP* II, p. 198.

51 'Les Choses de l'infini', *Phil* II, p. 601.

52 *William Shakespeare*, *Phil* II, pp. 220–31. See also Ann Jefferson, *Genius in France: An Idea and its Uses* (Princeton, NJ, 2015), pp. 81–7.

53 'To Jean Aicard', 17 November 1868, *CRP* III, p. 144.

54 *SP*, pp. 250–51 ('Réalité', I.2.ii).

55 *TS*, p. 299.

56 'To Armand Barbès', 29 August 1868, *CRP* III, p. 136.

57 *L'Homme qui rit*, *Rom* VIII, p. 426.

5 'I am a man of revolution' (1870–85)

1 'À Meurice et Vacquerie', 28 April 1871, *AP* III, p. 113.

2 'Tout pardoner . . .', *L'Art d'être grand-père* (VI, x), *Pse* VIII, p. 480.

3 *La Légende des siècles* (XVII, ii), *Pse* V, p. 360.

4 'Rentrée à Paris', 5 September 1870, *AP* III, p. 36.

5 'Aux Allemands' and 'Aux Français', 9/17 September 1870, *AP* III, pp. 37–45.

6 'Aux Allemands', p. 44.

7 1 January 1871, *CV* II, p. 168.

8 Thiers used this formulation on 13 February 1850 in the Legislative Assembly.

9 25 March 1871, *CV* II, p. 187.

10 'À Meurice et Vacquerie', 28 April 1871, *CRP* III, p. 113.

11 'Un cri', 'Pas de représailles' and 'Les deux trophées', *L'Année terrible*, *Pse* VIII, pp. 144–9 and 157–62.

12 See Robert Tombs, 'How Bloody was *la Semaine sanglante* of 1871? A Revision', *Historical Journal*, LV/3 (2012), pp. 619–704, and John Merriman, *Massacre: The Life and Death of the Paris Commune of 1871* (New Haven, CT, 2014), pp. 224–52.

13 'L'Incident belge', 27 May 1871, *AP* III, p. 118.

14 *SP*, pp. 264–5 (*L'Année terrible*).

15 *L'Année terrible*, *Pse* VIII, pp. 197–8 and 204–7.

16 Ibid., 'À l'éveque qui m'appelle athée' and 'Épilogue', pp. 59–60 and 263–4.

17 Cited in Alain Decaux, *Victor Hugo* (Paris, 1984), p. 959.

18 *OC* (Laffont) XV, p. 332.

19 *SP*, pp. 252–3 ('Fuis l'Éden . . .', *Songs of the Streets and Woods*, I.4.ix).

20 Cited in Michel de Decker, *Hugo: Victor, pour ces dames* (Paris, 2002), p. 208.

21 *SP*, pp. 398–9 ('Les Mangeurs', *La Légende des siècles*, XXXIII, vi).

22 *JD*, 28 July 1874.

23 *Mes Fils* (viii), *AP* III, p. 673.

24 'To Alphonse Karr', 8 January 1874, *CRP* IV, p. 2.

25 *Quatrevingt-treize*, *Rom* IX, p. 200.

26 'Le Droit et la loi' (x, 1875), *AP* I, p. 29.

27 'Pour la Serbie', 30 August 1876, *AP* III, p. 257.

28 Georges Hugo, *Mon Grand-père* (Paris, 1902), pp. 7–10.

29 'Parfois . . .', *L'Art d'être grand-père* (I, vii), *Pse* VIII, p. 416.

30 'Oh! Comme ils sont goulus!', ibid. (III, iv), p. 435.

31 Ibid. (VI, vi), p. 474.

32 *Histoire d'un crime*, *Hst* I, pp. 389–90.

33 *Pse* IX, pp. 65–8.

34 'Le Centenaire de Voltaire' (30 May 1878); 'Discours d'ouverture, Congrès littéraire international' (21 June 1878), *AP* III, pp. 301 and 312.

35 *JD*, 13 January 1874.

36 Henri Guillemin, *Hugo et la sexualité* (Paris, 1954), p. 134.

37 *La Pitié suprême* (x), *Pse* IX, p. 134.

38 *Religions et Religion* (v), *Pse* IX, p. 254.

39 *L'Âne* (i), *Pse* IX, p. 305.

40 *SP*, pp. 308–9 ('Pensées de nuit', *Les Quatre vents*, III, xlii).

41 *JD*, 26 February 1882.

42 *OC* (Laffont) XV, pp. 334 and 265.

43 *EVH*, pp. 326–7 ('Pendant une maladie', *Chansons des rues et des bois*, II.4.ii).

6 'I will be closing my eyes, but . . .' (Post-1885)

1 31 August 1881, available at: http://expositions.bnf.fr/hugo/grand/346.htm).

2 Cham, *Le Charivari*, 24 January 1871; cited in Pierre Georgel, *La Gloire de Victor Hugo* (Paris, 1985), p. 122.

3 *CV* (Juin), II, p. 772.

4 *La Légende des siècles* (XLIX, xii), *Pse* VI, pp. 266–7.

5 See Edward Breck's additional chapter in his translation of Alfred Barbou's *Victor Hugo and His Times* (Honolulu, HI, 2001), pp. 445–6.

6 Friedrich Nietzsche, *Twilight of the Idols*, trans. Duncan Large (Oxford, 1998), p. 43; and *Beyond Good and Evil*, trans. Marion Faber (Oxford, 1998), section 254.

7 'Ce que c'est que la mort', *Contemplations* (VI, xxii), *Pse* III, p. 388.

8 *Religions et Religion* (I, iii), *Pse* IX, p. 202.

9 'To Jules Janin', 2 September 1855, *CRP* II, p. 221.

10 *William Shakespeare*, *Phil* II, p. 176.

11 *Mis*, p. 243.

12 Ibid., p. 146.

13 The polls were conducted by *Le Magazine littéraire* and the newspaper *Le Figaro* in February and March 2015; Macron's comments came in an interview with the magazine *Historia* and were reported by the weekly *L'Obs* on 21 March 2017 (www.nouvelobs.com).

14 In August 2017, Google's search engine returned these results (rounded to the nearest million): Victor Hugo (65); Jane Austen (25); Mark Twain

(33); Balzac (14), Jules Verne (15), Emile Zola (1), and *Les Misérables* (13 – the variance for returns related to the abbreviation *Les Miz* is negligible). Even when adding the qualifier 'France' to Hugo's name, which potentially eliminates hits for individuals named after him but might also sideline valid links, the result was 24 million.

15 'Promontorium Somnii', *Phil* II, p. 310.

Conclusion

1 Aline Leclerc, 'Place de la République, Brel, Hugo et Hallyday en hommage aux victimes des attentats', www.lemonde.fr, 10 January 2016.

2 See Renaud Artoux, 'Alexane Ozier-Lafontaine: quand la jeunesse interroge son histoire', www.afrik.com, 1 September 2017.

3 'Discours sur l'Afrique', 18 May 1879, *AP* III, p. 330.

4 Hugo wrote of his works as 'an indivisible whole' in 1859; Jean-Marc Hovasse, *Victor Hugo, pendant l'exil 1851–64* (Paris, 2008), p. 573.

5 'To Madame Octave Giraud', 20 January 1867, *CRP* III, p. 3.

6 'To Léon Hugonnet', 24 August 1869, *CRP* III, p. 216.

7 Franck Laurent's *Victor Hugo face à la conquête de l'Algérie* (Paris, 2001) extensively addresses Hugo's uneasy relationship with colonialism. Similarly, Jennifer Yee's *Exotic Subversions in Nineteenth-century French Fiction* (Oxford, 2008) discusses how French writers troubled imperialist supremacy, including Hugo in *Bug-Jargal*.

8 'Ce que vous appelez . . .', *Toute la lyre* (III, xx), *Pse* XII, p. 189.

9 See my article '"Chateaubriand ou rien, Hugo et tout": Contemplating the Poet's Posterity', *Dix-neuf*, XX/3–4 (2016), pp. 229–40, and Marie-Hélène Léotin, 'A propos de Victor Hugo', www.martinique. franceantilles.fr, 31 May 2017.

10 Cited in Peter Brooks, *Flaubert in the Ruins of Paris* (New York, 2017), p. 63.

Select Bibliography

Hugo's Writings in French

Hugo's complete works are available in three main series:

Œuvres complètes (éditions Ollendorff et Albin Michel; Imprimerie nationale), ed. Paul Meurice (1904–5), Gustave Simon (1905–28) and Cécile Daubray (1933–52), 45 vols (Paris, 1902–52)
Œuvres complètes (édition chronologique Club français du Livre), ed. Jean Massin, 18 vols (Paris, 1967–70)
Œuvres complètes (éditions Robert Laffont), ed. Jacques Seebacher and Guy Rosa, 18 vols (Paris, 1985–2002)

Many of his works are also available from Gallimard, in both their Folio Classique and Pléiade collections.

A Selection of Works by Hugo in English Translation

Bug-Jargal [1826], trans. Chris Bongie (Peterborough, ON, 2004)
Cromwell [1826–7], trans. George Burnham Ives, ebook (Boston, MA, 1909)
Drawings by Victor Hugo, ed. Pierre Georgel (London, 1974)
The Essential Victor Hugo, trans. E. H. and A. M. Blackmore (Oxford, 2004)
Hans of Iceland [1823], trans. George Burnham Ives, ebook (Boston, MA, 1894)
The Last Day of a Condemned Man: and Other Prison Writings, trans. Geoff Woollen (Oxford, 1992)
The Man Who Laughs [1869], trans. Isabel F. Hapgood, ebook (New York, 1888)
Les Misérables [1862], trans. Julie Rose (London, 2008)

Napoleon the Little [1852], trans. George Burnham Ives, ebook
    (Boston, MA, 1909)
Ninety-three [1874], trans. Lowell Bair (New York, 1962)
Notre-Dame de Paris [1831], trans. John Sturrock (London, 2004)
The Rhine [1842], trans. David Mitchell Aird, ebook (London, 1843)
Selected Poems of Victor Hugo: A Bilingual Edition, trans. E. H. and
    A. M. Blackmore (Chicago, IL, 2001)
The Toilers of the Sea [1866], trans. James Hogarth (New York, 2002)
*Victor Hugo – Four Plays: Marion de Lorme, Hernani, Lucrezia Borgia, Ruy
    Blas*, ed. Claude Schumacher, trans. John Golder, Richard J. Hand
    and William D. Howarth (London, 2004)
Victor Hugo: Selected Poetry, trans. Steven Monte (New York, 2002)
William Shakespeare [1864], trans. Melville B. Anderson, ebook (London, 1910)

A wide range of Hugo's drawings and decors, along with photographs, memorabilia, illustrations, portraits and manuscripts, can be viewed in English at the Maisons de Victor Hugo's collection website (www.maisonsvictorhugo.paris.fr). These collections are held by the two Hugo museums at his former homes at the Place des Vosges in Paris and at Hauteville House in Guernsey. Hugo's graphic works can also be viewed at the Bibliothèque nationale de France inviting online exhibition (http://expositions.bnf.fr/hugo).

Biographical Works on Hugo

Barbou, Alfred, *Victor Hugo and His Times*, trans. Edward Breck
    (Honolulu, HI, 2001)
Davidson, A. F., *Victor Hugo: His Life and Work* (London, 1912)
Decaux, Alain, *Victor Hugo* (Paris, 1984)
Fillipetti, Sandrine, *Victor Hugo* (Paris, 2011)
Gallo, Max, *Victor Hugo*, 2 vols (Paris, 2001)
Grant, Elliott M., *The Career of Victor Hugo* (Cambridge, MA, 1945)
Grossiord, Sophie, *Victor Hugo: 'Et s'il n'en reste qu'un . . .'* (Paris, 1998)
Hovasse, Jean-Marc, *Victor Hugo, avant l'exil 1802–51* (Paris, 2001)
—, *Victor Hugo, pendant l'exil 1851–64* (Paris, 2008)
Hugo, Adèle, *Victor Hugo raconté par un témoin de sa vie* (Brussels, 1863)
Hugo, Georges, *Mon Grand-père* (Paris, 1902)

Juin, Hubert, *Victor Hugo*, 3 vols (Paris, 1980–86)

Maurois, André, *Olympio, ou la vie de Victor Hugo* (Paris, 1954)

Richardson, Joanna, *Victor Hugo* (London, 1976)

Robb, Graham, *Victor Hugo* (London, 1997)

Stein, Marieke, *Victor Hugo* (Paris, 2007)

Works on Hugo's Writing

Albouy, Pierre, *La Création mythologique chez Victor Hugo* (Paris, 1963)

Audinet, Gérard, and Vincent Gille, eds, *Éros Hugo: entre pudeur et excès*, exh. cat., Maison de Victor Hugo (Paris, 2015)

Barnett, Marva, *Victor Hugo on Things that Matter* (New Haven, CT, 2009)

Barrère, Jean-Bertrand, *Victor Hugo à l'œuvre: le poète en exil et en voyage* (Paris, 1970)

Baudouin, Charles, *Psychanalyse de Victor Hugo* [1943], ed. Pierre Albouy (Paris, 1972)

Bellos, David, *The Novel of the Century: The Extraordinary Adventure of Les Misérables* (London, 2017)

Brombert, Victor, *Victor Hugo and the Visionary Novel* (Cambridge, MA, 1985)

Chambers, John, *Victor Hugo's Conversations with the Spirit World* (New York, 2008)

Charles, David, *La Pensée technique dans l'œuvre de Victor Hugo: le bricolage de l'infini* (Paris, 1997)

Cox, Fiona, 'Les Misérables: The Shadowlands of Epic', in *Haunting Presences*, ed. Kate Griffiths and David Evans (Cardiff, 2009), pp. 75–88

Decker, Michel de, *Hugo: Victor, pour ces dames* (Paris, 2002)

Frey, John Andrew, *A Victor Hugo Encyclopaedia* (Westport, CT, 1999)

Garval, Michael D., 'Victor Hugo: The Writer as Monument', in *A Dream of Stone: Fame, Vision, and Monumentality in Nineteenth-century French Literary Culture* (Newark, NJ, 2004), pp. 158–206

Gaudon, Jean, ed., *Victor Hugo: Lettres à Juliette Drouet* (Paris, 1964)

—, *Le Temps de la contemplation: l'œuvre poétique de Victor Hugo des 'Misères' au 'Seuil du gouffre', 1845–56* (Paris, 1969)

Gémie, Sharif, 'The Republic, the People, and the Writer: Victor Hugo's Political and Social Writing', *French History*, XIV/3 (2000), pp. 272–94

Georgel, Pierre, *La Gloire de Victor Hugo* (Paris, 1985)

—, Delphine Gleizes, Stéphane Guégan and Ségolène le Man, eds,
   L'Œil de Victor Hugo (Paris, 2004)

Gleizes, Delphine, ed., *L'Œuvre de Victor Hugo à l'écran: des rayons et des
   ombres* (Québec, City, 2005)

Grant, Richard B., *The Perilous Quest: Image, Myth, and Prophecy in the
   Narratives of Victor Hugo* (Durham, NC, 1968)

Grossman, Kathryn M., *The Early Novels of Victor Hugo: Towards a Poetics
   of Harmony* (Geneva, 1985)

—, *Figuring Transcendence in 'Les Misérables': Hugo's Romantic Sublime*
   (Carbondale, IL, 1994)

—, *'Les Misérables': Conversion, Revolution, Redemption* (New York, 1996)

—, *The Later Novels of Victor Hugo: Variations on the Politics and Poetics of
   Transcendence* (Oxford, 2012)

—, and Bradley Stephens, eds, *Les Misérables and its Afterlives: Between Page,
   Stage, and Screen* (London, 2015)

Guerlac, Suzanne, *The Impersonal Sublime: Hugo, Baudelaire, Lautréamont*
   (Stanford, CA, 1990)

Guillemin, Henri, *Hugo et la sexualité* (Paris, 1954)

Halsall, Albert W., *Victor Hugo and the Romantic Drama* (Toronto, 1998)

Hiddleston, J. A., ed., *Victor Hugo, romancier de l'abîme* (Oxford, 2002)

Hugo, Marie, Laura and Jean-Baptiste, *Hauteville House:
   Victor Hugo, décorateur* (Paris, 2016)

Ireson, J. C., *Victor Hugo: A Companion to his Poetry* (Oxford, 1997)

Laster, Arnaud, *Pleins feux sur Victor Hugo* (Paris, 1981)

Laurent, Franck, *Victor Hugo face à la conquête de l'Algérie* (Paris, 2001)

Léotin, Marie-Hélène, 'A propos de Victor Hugo', www.martinique.
   franceantilles.fr, 31 May 2017

Makki, Laura El and Guillaume Gallienne, *Un Été avec Victor Hugo*
   (Paris, 2016)

Maurel, Jean, *Victor Hugo philosophe* (Paris, 1985)

Mehlman, Jeffrey, *Revolution and Repetition: Marx, Hugo, Balzac*
   (Berkeley, CA, 1977)

Meschonnic, Henri, *Pour la poétique IV: Écrire Hugo* (Paris, 1977)

Morisi, Ève, 'Putting Pain to Paper: Victor Hugo's New Abolitionist Poetics',
   in *Death Sentences: Literature and State Killing*, ed. Birte Christ and Ève
   Morisi (Oxford, 2019)

Naugrette, Florence, *Le Théâtre de Victor Hugo* (Lausanne, 2016)

Ousselin, Edward, 'Victor Hugo's European Utopia', *Nineteenth-century French Studies*, XXXIV/1 (2005), pp. 32–43

Pena-Ruiz, Henri and Jean-Paul Scot, *Un Poète en politique: les combats de Victor Hugo* (Paris, 2002)

Petrey, Sandy, *History in the Text: 'Quatrevingt-treize' and the French Revolution* (West Lafayette, IN, 1981)

Piroué, Georges, *Victor Hugo romancier, ou les dessus de l'inconnu* (Paris, 1964)

Porter, Laurence M., *Victor Hugo* (Boston, MA, 1999)

Prévost, Marie-Laure, *Le Cahier 'Victor Hugo, l'homme océan'* (Paris, 2002)

Raser, Timothy, *The Simplest of Signs: Victor Hugo and the Language of Images in France, 1850–1950* (Newark, NJ, 2004)

Roche, Isabel, *Character and Meaning in the Novels of Victor Hugo* (West Lafayette, IN, 2007)

Roman, Myriam, *Victor Hugo et le roman philosophique* (Paris, 1999)

Rosa, Guy and Anne Ubersfeld, eds, *Lire 'Les Misérables'* (Paris, 1985)

Savy, Nicole, 'Victus, sed Victor (1852–1862)', in *En collaboration avec le soleil: Victor Hugo, photographies de l'exil*, ed. Françoise Heilbrun and Danielle Molinari (Paris, 1999), pp. 16–39

—, *Le Paris de Hugo* (Paris, 2016)

Stein, Marieke, *Victor Hugo, orateur politique* (Paris, 2007)

Stephens, Bradley, '*Baisez-moi, belle Juju!* Victor Hugo and the Joy of his Juliette', in *'Joie de vivre' in French Literature and Culture*, ed. Susan Harrow and Timothy Unwin (Amsterdam, 2009), pp. 211–24

—, *Victor Hugo, Jean-Paul Sartre, and the Liability of Liberty* (Oxford, 2011)

—, '"Chateaubriand ou rien, Hugo et tout": Contemplating the Poet's Posterity', *Dix-neuf*, XX/3–4 (2016), pp. 229–40

—, 'The Novel and the [Il]Legibility of History: Victor Hugo, Honoré de Balzac, and Alexandre Dumas', in *The Oxford Handbook to European Romanticism*, ed. Paul Hamilton (Oxford, 2016), pp. 88–104

Vacquerie, Auguste, *Profils et grimaces* (Paris, 1856)

Yee, Jennifer, 'Victor Hugo and the Other as Divided Self in *Bug-Jargal*', in J. Yee, *Exotic Subversions in Nineteenth-century French Fiction* (Oxford, 2008), pp. 45–62

Zarifopol-Johnston, Illinca, *To Kill a Text: The Dialogic Fiction of Hugo, Dickens, and Zola* (Newark, NJ, 1995)

The website of the Paris-based Groupe Hugo offers up-to-date resources for publications, conferences, events and exhibitions (http://groupugo.div.jussieu.fr/Default.htm).

Acknowledgements

My thanks go first and foremost to my editor at Reaktion, Vivian Constantinopoulos, not only for the invitation to write this biography but also for her support and guidance throughout its development. Other members of the editorial team who helped polish the text when it transitioned into print include Reaktion's managing editor Aimee Selby, who gave much-needed help with arranging the referencing system during production, as well as both Matt Milton and Phoebe Colley.

I have been very fortunate to discuss my ideas for this book with a range of Hugo-inspired colleagues. These include Arnaud Laster, Danièle Gasiglia-Laster and the Société des Amis de Victor Hugo; Marie-Laure Marco and Michèle Berteaux at the Maison de Victor Hugo's library in Paris, as well as the museum's director Gérard Audinet (who was also enormously helpful with identifying and obtaining many of the images in this book); members of the Groupe Hugo research network, including Jean-Marc Hovasse, Claude Millet and Florence Naugrette; and the Victor Hugo in Guernsey Society (especially Roy Bisson and Dinah Bott) and the Guernsey Arts Commission, as well as the chief administrator at Hauteville House, Odile Blanchette, and her whole team, who all extended me a very warm welcome during research trips to the island in 2017 and 2018.

I am especially grateful to Kathryn Grossman for her insightful feedback on an early draft and for the many discussions we have had about Hugo over the years. In both respects, her input has been invaluable.

Conversations with academics working in French studies were also helpful in setting Hugo within context, including members of the Society for French Studies (SFS), the Society of Dix-Neuviémistes (SDN) and the Nineteenth-Century French Studies Association (NCFS) at each group's annual international conferences.

The Faculty of Arts at the University of Bristol generously awarded me an extra semester of research leave in 2017–18, which enabled me to finish this project and to lay the groundwork for further research related to Hugo. Also essential to this book's completion were my students at Bristol. Their perceptive readings of Hugo's work – and of French literature and culture more broadly – have continued to inform my own.

Various friends and family members have indulged my interests in Hugo throughout the writing process. Special thanks go to Andrea and P. J. Beaghton for their enthusiasm and generosity, and to Anthony Tromans, who – as ever – has been constantly encouraging and exceptionally patient. This book is dedicated to our nephews, nieces and godsons.

Photo Acknowledgements

The author and publishers wish to express their thanks to the below sources of illustrative material and/or permission to reproduce it.

The Artchives / Alamy Stock Photo: p. 111; © Bibliothèque nationale de France: pp. 125, 139, 150; © Maisons de Victor Hugo: pp. 56, 62, 73, 86, 90, 180; © Maisons de Victor Hugo / age fotostock / Alamy Stock Photo: p. 126; © Maisons de Victor Hugo / Heritage Image Partnership Ltd / Alamy Stock Photo: pp. 10, 16, 130; © Maisons de Victor Hugo / Photo 12 / Alamy Stock Photo: p. 129; © Maisons de Victor Hugo / Roger-Viollet: pp. 38, 39, 83, 116, 127, 128, 131, 132; Photo 12 / Alamy Stock Photo: p. 115; © Priaulx Library, Guernsey: pp. 124, 144, 153, 176; photo by Bradley Stephens: p. 123; WENN UK / Alamy Stock Photo: p. 193.